Ray Pittman takes you on an adrenaline-laced journey into real life experiences and exploits of living overseas. The story of his spiritual pilgrimage will not only captivate your attention, but also stimulate your spirit. Highly recommend!

—*Jeff Kinley, author of* As It Was In the Days of Noah

Some people write stories; others live a life that is worth writing about. Ray Pittman does both.

—*Adam Donyes, Founder/President Kanakuk Link Year*

Ray's journey will leave you breathless, inspired and motivated to see the world in a different way. This is the way of love, hope, friendship and faith–like a fire on the shore that will lead you across the ocean to safety, even when the sharks come.

—*Melinda Estabrooks, TV, podcast, web show host &*
international speaker

Ray Pittman's dramatic story shows how the real fun begins when God–the ultimate adventurer–takes the helm. Get ready for a stormy journey of laughter and tears that will carry you to distant worlds.

—*Steve Richardson, President, Pioneers USA*

Ray is the real deal. Not the average deal, but real. Real struggles, real triumphs, real desire to be used by God. This book of stories traces a path of relentless adventure and his journey toward God through thick and thin, through risk and reward, through the conflicts that many people have to sort out as they discover God for themselves.

—*Ron Snell, author of* The Rani Adventure Series

I have heard Ray tell stories of life in the Pacific for many years. His life and grand adventures have always confronted my lifestyle. Each of the chapters in this book is a challenge to live life more fully. Each chapter is an adventure to read in itself.

—*Mark Roche, Director of Homes of Hope Fiji*

WHEN THE SHARKS COME

WHEN THE SHARKS COME

RAY PITTMAN

Manila

Philippines

Pacific
Ocean

Blak

Lake
Holmes

Papua
New
Guinea

Lombok

Indonesia

Outside Beach

Depapre

Mt. Cyclops

Sentani

Australia

print ISBN: 978-1-938633-82-9
ebook ISBN: 978-1-938633-83-6

re·tell·ing
Produced by Retelling
www.Retelling.net

in association with Samizdat Creative
www.samizdatcreative.com

Cover design by Laura Pittman
Cover drone image of Coral Coast reef in Fiji. All rights Ray
Pittman 2017.
Map by Kaelin M. Groom, PhD. All copyrights reserved © 2017

Ray Pittman may be contacted at fijifam@gmail.com

CONTENTS

DEDICATION

With sincere love I'd like to dedicate this book to the following:

My mother Linda, who passed away before she had a chance to read it. You always believed in me more than I believed in myself. You gave me the courage and inspiration to try things that I was afraid to fail at because you never doubted me for a second. There are so many things I would love to share with you that I can't now, this book being one of them.

My wife Laura and three daughters, Eden, Elani and Isla. You bring me joy and comfort. I have absolutely loved the adventure of being a husband and a dad. I would swim through an ocean full of sharks for you! These stories are for you so that you never forget me.

Uncle Wally, you changed my life by including me in your family and adventures. Thanks for always being transparent and genuine. For asking me hard questions and for taking the time to show me how Jesus was real and relevant, and how to live for him. I'll never forget our beach campouts, spearfishing, dive trips, exploring and long talks around the campfire. Don't ever forget I saved your life when you nearly drowned laughing at me that time when the parrotfish bit me in the butt.

To all the third culture kids who grew up in countries that weren't your passport country, I know the struggles you have faced and I know how it feels. Every chapter is a new beginning, this world is not our home. The only place you might find to belong is in stories that might sound to some like fiction. But we'll find each other there in those grand adventures and we'll recognize each other as from the same tribe.

Finally to all you wanderers who long to see over the horizon, who are unsettled with life as it is and want more. I pray you will never stop searching until you find what you're looking for. This book is for you, may it light your way.

PROLOGUE

In the Fiji Islands there are many legends about the shark god named *Dakuwaqa* (da-ku-wanga). This ancient god of the old island religion has the ability to shape shift to the form of either man or shark, or half-man, half-shark. *Dakuwaqa* is the unpredictable ancestral guardian of the maze of reefs that lie under the turquoise waters in Fiji to the north, and the protector of the highest Chief of Cakaudrove province.

The high chiefs of this province are considered by some to be descendants of *Dakuwaqa* and recipients at times of his power and protection. Traditionally known as totem god to these chiefs, this shark god could both be protector or aggressor depending upon what offense you may have committed against him or the chief.

To this day, villagers tell many tales of personal encounters with *Dakuwaqa*. It had been widely rumored that three of my neighbors offended *Dakuwaqa* in some manner, by not adhering to traditional taboos, beliefs and practices. Unfortunately the three of them were mysteriously and tragically dismembered by sharks in the past year. One lost a leg, another a chunk of his side, and one had his head

1

bitten off by a shark while spearfishing.

But I wasn't worried about that.

Not yet anyway.

> *"When the sharks come, you really pray from the heart!"*
> —Jione Tiu ("Apa John" Rotuman Fisherman)

PIRATES

The sun blinded me as it reflected off the ocean like a mirror. I narrowed my eyes and squinted into the bright light. In spite of the fact it was a glorious calm morning in the South Pacific, danger was headed in my direction.

Anyone who makes a life on the sea is tuned in to nature; you have to be, your life could depend on it. You don't want to be caught in the open sea with three quarters of an inch of fiberglass between you and Davy Jones' locker when a storm materializes out of nowhere. No, you read the rhythm of the waves, the feel of the salty wind in your face, the pounding, pulsing surf, the slightest change in humidity, the clouds and the pastel colors of the sky. You must have a sixth sense for the nature around you. Is everything doing what it's supposed to be doing or is one thing off? All was perfect on this particular day and I breathed it in deeply. I breathed it in right down into my soul, as the *Buckaroo* bobbed up and down in the waves.

I had just purposely marooned a group of American university students on an isolated beach. They had been in Fiji only a couple of weeks before I woke them up at 4 a.m., loaded them into the boat with the clothes on their backs, and dropped them off on this desolate beach for a week. I'd left them with a bagful of items they may possibly have had if they had been truly shipwrecked: odd pieces of rope, tangled up fishing line, a few hooks, a couple matches, some mismatched snorkel gear, a local fish spear, some water and other odds and ends. This experience was part of a three-and-a-half month long adventure and community development study-abroad program my wife and I were directing at the time.

The students would remain on the deserted beach for a week to learn survival skills from an old Rotuman fisherman, John Tiu, or Apa (which means "father" in his native language). Apa's home country, Rotuma, is a Polynesian island floating around in the middle of nowhere, closest to the nation of Fiji. This beautiful and unique people group has been adopted by Fiji although they maintain their own Rotuman language and culture. While survival would be part of the students' experience, the greater lesson here was to learn respect for someone who may not have been wealthy in a traditional sense, but incredibly rich in many others— like possessing the knowledge and experience to comfortably live off the sea. They would discover Apa John had actually been shipwrecked so many times he could make a holiday out of the situation.

Because we lived and operated the study-abroad program off the grid, it was necessary to make a weekly boat trip to stock up on food, groceries, fuel, supplies, kerosene, and mail. The remote 50-acre coconut plantation we were living on was cut off from road access by mountains and sea. To reach the nearest town on our island it would take several hours, the first leg by boat and the rest of the way several hours down the unpaved Hibiscus Highway, so it was easier to cross the Somosomo Strait by boat to the neighboring island of Taveuni. The third largest of Fiji's more than 300 islands, Taveuni, or the Garden Island as it is called, is a lush, picturesque island directly east of us known for its diving, waterfalls, and exotic flora and fauna. During the time of our study-abroad programs, the Garden Island also had a fuel depot, a post office and an Indian owned supermarket—just a round-trip boat ride away to buy everything we needed to meet our basic needs.

The trip would take about forty-five minutes in calm conditions and as long as three hours in bad weather. There were days the sea was like glass and there were days when the waves were twenty feet high. You would either love it or hate it.

The Somosomo Strait had a bit of a reputation at the time for being sharky. Some said it was because the butcher in Taveuni threw animal entrails into the sea, others said it was because of *Dakuwaqa* and some said it was all superstition. Tell that to my dead neighbors, I suppose.

Living in shark infested waters, my neighbors on the small island north of our beach, the Kioans (Polynesians from Tuvalu who had been relocated by the British to a neighboring island near the Somosomo Strait) attached an extra baton to their handmade canoes to smack sharks that came too close to their boats. One day I noticed a bite mark in my friend Pule's canoe and he said it was from a Mako shark out for a morning nibble when he paddled over to our bay. Sharks use their mouths to figure out what things are, which has given them a bad reputation based on the misconception that they are mindless man eaters thanks to many Hollywood misrepresentations. Nevertheless superstitious fishermen would pour a bowl of kava (the traditional drink in Fiji made from the root of a pepper plant) into the sea as offering to *Dakuwaqa* for protection. Those who believed in the Christian God prayed to him for safety. Those who didn't believe in either took their chances I suppose.

The best time to cross the Somosomo Strait was first thing in the morning when the sun was high enough to see the submerged reefs and the water was still calm enough to cross safely and comfortably. With my to-do list in hand, I maneuvered the *Buckaroo* carefully into the reef passage at Udukacu (Oon-doo-ka-thoo). Gretchen, a good friend who worked with us on staff, was with me to run our routine errands. Underwater, adorned with a rainbow of multicolored living organisms, the channel cut through the high coral walls like a large Z. The *Buckaroo* handled the rising and falling of the waves perfectly while it sliced through the tight turns like an old pro. It had taken me at least a year to create a mental map of the underwater reef system that ran through the northern frontiers of the Fiji Islands. A keen eye, a steady hand and a captain's knowledge of the reefs were crucial for safety in these waters. When it comes to the ocean you have to do whatever you can to be safe, but at the end of the day you're still at its mercy.

I waited offshore for a check-in with Apa to be sure the students were in satisfactory condition and that no one needed to be evacuated. This check-in was a daily practice we followed throughout "survival week." Apa paddled out in a dugout outrigger canoe to meet us and assured me everyone was settling in okay. I scanned the beach to see if the students were busy making shelters or fire, but to my dismay they were simply lounging on the beach like driftwood. I always thought to myself if I had that opportunity I would have built myself a tropical palace by now, with a deck, thatched roof, bamboo floors, table, chairs, a bed, something worthy of Blue Lagoon fame.

Satisfied enough with Apa's report that my students were safe and sound, I turned the *Buckaroo* east and headed for Taveuni. I never worried about anyone I left with Apa. The man would give his life for them in a second if he had to. I knew that by the end of the week, the students would love Apa as a father just as his name portrays. And not just love him, but respect him deeply.

Out of the passage, I checked my visual bearings with the usual landmarks on Taveuni and my position relative to Vanua Levu (the island to my starboard side) and pushed down the throttle, only to look up and see a red and white open fiberglass boat, typical of the village boats that roamed these waters, rapidly approaching me from the Somosomo Strait. I didn't recognize the markings or the men on board and concluded they weren't from our bay. I turned to port to make way for them—they turned to intercept me. I swerved starboard and they turned again, coming straight for my bow at high speed.

"What is going on?" I muttered.

Something wasn't right.

Soon I could see their faces as they approached, and they

weren't friendly, a group of eight village youth who seemed to be bearing down on me with a vengeance.

"Great." I wiped my brow with the back of my hand. "Pirates." The sarcastic groan slipped out under my breath.

I didn't dare tell Gretchen, the beautiful strawberry blonde who sat unaware by my side. Gretchen was dragging her hand through the warm, crystal clear water, enjoying everything good and beautiful about Fiji, which was in her nature. Fiji waters are generally friendly and pirate free. Long gone are the days when this place was known as the Cannibal Isles, when human flesh was a regular staple of the Fijian diet. We no longer have pirates like most people envision them.

What we had here were thugs in a speedboat with what seemed to me pirate-like intentions. Fiji has had its fare share of unsavory characters in the past. In the years of early European exploration when men were travelling the globe by ship seeking their fortunes, many white men had jumped ship in these islands. They were black birders (men looking to make money off slaves), whalers who had had enough of the sea and wanted to settle down with an island bride, adventure seekers, and entrepreneurs looking to make a fortune from logging sandalwood or harvesting *beche-de-mer* (delicacy sea creatures with alleged restorative properties, basically a sea slug) from the ocean. Some of the original European beachcombers had been shipwrecked and made their home on the island, being embraced by the local people that resulted in quite a few half-caste landowners with English names generations later. A few of the less noble seafarers were so entranced by the tropical islands that they jumped ship, or even worse, mutinied and murdered the captain and crew so they could remain in paradise and keep the goods at the same time. Over the years, the pirate antics of the beach-combers' descendants have calmed down, but still.

Times had changed, but Fiji was still in turmoil. There had been a coup in recent years that the country was still recovering from. And there was another military coup looming on the horizon. I'm not an expert by any means on what was happening—generally we left these issues to the Fiji-ans—but the best I could understand was that at this time in Fiji's history a nationalistic movement had been fighting politically for *qoliqoli* (traditional fishing ground) rights for the indigenous people. The battle surrounding this partic-ular issue, and certainly much more complex issues—that Fijians comprehend better than I do—eventually led to an overthrow of the government by the military. That would come a year later, but at the moment a faction of villagers, believing that the *qoliqoli* bill was a done deal, were beginning to take matters into their own hands over what they consid-ered *their* waters. At that time there wasn't a clear definition of how to handle this, by any side, so people (especially in remote areas) were left to figure it out on their own. One thing was for sure, living in a remote and generally lawless region, there wasn't much hope of protection for us.

I had read a few stories in the paper of people being beaten and having their boats stolen, left to tread water or dumped on a beach. There had even been a recent story of one man who had been shot with a spear gun and left for dead. In all fairness, villagers had good reason to be con-cerned about their fishing grounds. Most villages located on the islands made their living from the sea. It is their livelihood and part of their traditional way of life for generations. With the recent influx of modern fishing equipment on long line boats and the incredible destructiveness of netting and shark finning, their resources were being depleted faster than ever. Villagers had to fish longer and harder for fewer and fewer results, making life more difficult, and understandably they weren't at all happy about it.

Piracy of village fishing grounds posed a real threat to these islanders' way of life. The Fijian government had stepped in to make it illegal to fish in tribal fishing grounds without the permission of the relevant traditional landowning tribes. This included the highly lucrative *beche-de-mer* that was being unscrupulously exploited with maximum greed. Many local *beche-de-mer* divers who were being hired by unethical operators were being subjected to unsafe diving conditions and there were far too many deaths associated with the business. Occasionally these operators would sneak into tribal waters in the dark of the night so as not to be detected by the rightful owners. Some of these divers disappeared and were never seen again. It is widely believed they were taken by sharks. Locals will tell you if you don't respect the sacred rights of the traditional chiefs or the sea under *Dakuwaqa's* protection, you could become shark bait.

It's a mystery that intrigued me, this shark god legend. Supposedly many years ago when the chief of Taveuni died, sharks escorted the ship that carried his body all the way through the Somosomo Strait to his burial spot. To this day, and to the best of my knowledge, out of respect of a chief who dies, fishing is prohibited for 100 days following his death. Now, I have an enormous respect for the sea and the Fijian people. I wasn't out there to exploit anyone's resources, but these guys bearing down on me in their red speedboat didn't know that, and it didn't look like they were going to ask. I had already learned that aggression in this culture was not a positive thing, and it was obvious I was about to become *aggressed* upon.

If that wasn't enough cause for worry, I had Gretchen with me. I have always been incredibly overprotective of people in my care and I wasn't about to let anything happen to her. I began to mentally prepare myself for the worst-case scenario.

It was obvious by their speed I couldn't outrun their boat in the old *Buckaroo*. My only chance was to outwit them. I spun the boat hard to port and pulled up near three large rocks that jutted up from the seafloor and lay just beneath the surface. They were infamous for knocking off boat propellers. This just might give me the opportunity I needed to get away.

If it appeared they meant to harm us, I would gun the motor and force the approaching boat into the submerged rocks below. The tide was perfect for it. If we were lucky, their propeller would strike a rock, sheer the pin, fly off and leave them stranded. I let out a sigh. If this worked it would be one for the movies.

I looked at Gretchen nervously as I throttled back to wait for the pirates. I was glad I was wearing sunglasses, lest my eyes tell stories I didn't want told. Gretchen didn't suspect anything was wrong, and I was hoping to keep it that way. If I had to, I'd make something up. Gretchen would believe me. I laughed to myself, remembering the time she was chasing baby chickens around the plantation. She had seen me walking by and shouted, "Hey Ray! How do you pick up chicks?"

I stopped for a minute and looked at her to see if she was serious. "You have to have the right lines!" I shouted back.

"What do you mean?" She asked, looking confused.

"Think about it!" I chuckled as I walked off.

A few minutes later I heard her laughing.

Back in the boat, it was time to go. I grabbed the throttle and put it into gear. Suddenly the engine sputtered and died.

"No, no, no. Not now…" I cursed the old Mercury. I turned the key and nothing happened. "Aaaargh…stupid budget cuts!" I growled.

The *Buckaroo* ran most of the time, but still needed a lot of work. On her maiden voyage the 14-foot aluminum hull had bucked like a wild bronco over the large swells, earning her the name *Buckaroo*. She was probably built in the 1970s, sort of like a small, retro, hippie Winnebago without wheels. As rambunctious as she was, time had taken its toll on the old girl.

I leapt to the back of the boat and yanked on the start cord, the red boat swiftly closing the gap between us. I pulled with all my might. I pulled and I pulled and I pulled. I hated it when outboard motors did this. Sweat stung my eyes. I had been here before, pulling the start cord for hours and biting my tongue. This time I had pirates bearing down on me, Gretchen to protect, students on the beach, and a great escape plan—except for a stupid engine that wouldn't start.

Whirr, whirr, whirr…nothing. The smell of oil and fuel filled my nostrils. I had flooded the engine. Desperately

I looked around for something to defend us with. Down behind the battery box we kept a club made of dense mangrove wood. Apa's son had crafted it to incapacitate the large fish we caught when deep-sea fishing. One good whack to the brain and the fish would shudder and die. You didn't want a giant fish flopping around the boat with treble hooks hanging out of its mouth. Apa found that out the hard way when one got lodged in his hand from a massive Walu.

As the village boat pulled up beside us, I saw the angry young men positioning themselves on the rails to board us. Adrenalin coursing through my veins, I reached for the club. It felt heavy and cold in my hand. I remember as a child my father talking to me about weapons. "Once you pick one up, you may be forced to use it," he'd warned. Could I go through with this if I had to? I wasn't sure.

I faked an innocent smile then turned and faced the pirates, the club hidden behind my right thigh. *Just another day at the office*, I grimaced. *Try to look at the bright side—this is certainly going to be interesting.*

I had looked into the eyes of death before. My life's journey had been a wild and stormy ride, but as the pirates leaned toward our vessel, a calm and serene peace washed over me. Today I was not afraid. If I were to walk, or swim, through the door that led to my final adventure, it would be okay. My dreams had come true and the desires of my heart had been fulfilled. There was nothing more I wished for, nothing more I was seeking and nothing more I could think to ask of the great God.

What the "pirates" didn't know is that death and I had already met, and my greatest adventure had already begun.

The boat slammed up against the *Buckaroo*.

I stood up on the gunwale.

"Who's feeling lucky today?" I challenged.

THE *LUCKY CATCH*

I was eleven years old the first time I saw a dead body. The boy was only nine, lying curled up in the bottom of an aluminum boat. His shoes were gone and he wore only one sock. His face was pale white, his lips purple and blue. His eyes were closed peacefully as if he were sleeping. I wanted to wake him up, but I knew that his soul had already been stolen away. As I looked down at him, I wondered where his spirit had gone. This wasn't the boy I had known a few hours before. This was just a shell, like an envelope without a letter.

The blue sky swirled with white clouds carelessly above me, completely ignoring the tragic drama unfolding below. Gently, I released minnows from a yellow bucket and watched them swim away without a thank you. What simple creatures, minnows, so unlucky to be created to be food for all the other fish. They shimmered silvery blue in the sun. Suddenly the fish scattered as a rescue boat careened up the boat ramp, sparks flying from the aluminum scraping against the concrete and jerked to a stop.

"Can you identify this boy?" the captain yelled at me,

pointing to the body.

I didn't flinch in spite of the growing fear inside me. I knew caffeine and adrenalin coursed through his veins, in mine only shock and denial. I put my hands on the cold wet rails of the aluminum boat and peered over the side. The boy with the blue lips should have been me. That should have been my lifeless body in the boat.

A second boat skidded up the ramp with a black body bag on the deck.

"Well? Do you know this boy?" the first man barked at me again.

I nodded.

The other man unzipped the body bag revealing the pale and blue face of another boy. "Do you know this one?" he demanded.

I nodded, "That's his brother, he's eleven, like me…" I trailed off, barely able to hear my own voice. Somewhere their mother had no idea that she would never see her sons alive again, her two beautiful boys. It was too tragic for me to take in. That very morning they had been alive. We had been talking together. We had been playing together. Why?

Dan, a family friend and former elementary school teacher of mine, ran up behind me. "What's the matter with you?" he snapped at the novice volunteer rescuers. "You don't ask a kid to identify bodies!" He pulled me away from the morbid scene and told me to run back to the cabin. I glanced back as Dan looked into the boat, his broad shoulders sank and he sobbed.

The remote fishing lodge and campground where we were staying was suddenly swarming with media crews, helicopters, police, and rescue volunteers. As I retreated through the tall pine trees and dirt roads to our cabin, dodging ambulances, policemen, news vans and people running with walkie-talkies, I began to piece together the events of the day.

Everything had happened so quickly. It felt like a dream—no, a surreal nightmare.

Every fifth year our family would leave Southeast Asia for a furlough in America for a year. It was normal for us to travel across America visiting our family and friends we hadn't seen in a long time. This year when we reached Minnesota in late summer, an old friend invited my dad, my brother and me to join a guys' adventure into Canada. We would be staying at a quaint little fishing camp by a lake in the forest. Seeing this as an opportunity to do something with his sons, he accepted the invitation and my dad, my younger brother Jeff, and I packed our bags for the weekend camping/fishing trip. We joined up with a group of guys Dan knew and made the long drive north.

When our fishing party awoke to the beauty of the Canadian wilderness that fateful morning, we were greeted by unseasonably cold weather: grey, dark, and raining. For me having been born and raised in the tropics, I wasn't enthusiastic about the chilly weather. I didn't like bundling up in multiple layers of clothes, buttoning up a heavy coat or wearing shoes and socks. Clothes weighed me down and depressed me. I rebelled against clothes but in this case I conceded it was a necessary evil.

Several of the men wandered out on the porch with their coffee cups to have a look at the sky, expressing a little disappointment about the weather conditions. But hey, this was a father/son fishing trip, we had come all this way, so everyone wanted to make the best of it. It was our second day on the lake and I was relieved to see that I would get to be aboard the *Lucky Catch*, a comfortable and spacious fishing boat, thrilled at not having to sit out in the miserable weather in an exposed dinghy. We packed a lunch and a cooler for our drinks, and gathered up our fishing gear.

At the last minute, as I was finishing my breakfast in the dining room, the nine-year-old boy approached me and asked to trade places on the boats for the day. He wanted to fish with his dad who had been assigned to the bigger boat, he said. The *Lucky Catch* was much nicer than the other cramped 12-ft aluminum dinghies. Everyone wanted to ride in the cushy boat with built-in ice chests, comfy seats and cup holders, so the leaders had made a sign-up rotation to be a *Lucky Catch* passenger. I was excited that it was finally my turn, but he was insistent and grudgingly I conceded.

The group had been in good spirits, laughing and joking over toast, bacon and eggs. The smell of strong coffee and the comfortable chatter of camaraderie drifted through the lodge, yet no one could have imagined that a few hours later seven people from around that table would be dead.

~ ~ ~ ~ ~

"My line's caught in the tree!" one fisherman hollered.

"Well, pull on it harder," the others in the small dinghy joked. "Are you trying to catch birds or fish?"

My dad, Jeff, Dan, and I watched from a distance in our own boat, chuckling as the guys gave their tangled friend a hard time. My friend Aaron, who was my age, was the only boy in their dinghy. He hadn't been as lucky as the other boy who had managed to trade for a spot on the luxurious *Lucky Catch*. The little dinghy was beginning to rock precariously while the men tried to free the line. Aaron looked over at me, rolled his eyes and lifted his arms in a comical imitation of the men. I smiled. He was such a clown, always making people laugh.

Suddenly, the men working the tangled line lost their balance, the boat tipped sharply and then capsized. Everyone let out a yelp as they plunged into the frigid lake water. The four of us snapped to attention and shifted in our seats. We reeled in our lines, ready to help but suddenly nervous about our boat.

The shore was too rocky and full of brambles for them to climb out. They stumbled, slipped and lunged for branches. Dan frowned, turned our boat toward them, and carefully motored over to the rescue.

"Okay, everyone grab hold of the rails, but don't try to get in, you'll capsize us too!" Dan ordered. The boat was barely large enough for the four of us. "Hold on, we'll tow you to shore."

Aaron's teeth chattered, "H-h-hey, my RC c-c-cola is floating a-a-away!"

"Don't worry," I said as I patted his cold hands. "I'll net it for you on our way back. It will stay icy cold in this freezing water. Hey, at least I'll be able to say I caught something!" We laughed.

Just then the *Lucky Catch* came zooming into the bay.

"Hooray!" we all cheered. "We're rescued!"

The four wet fishermen flopped into the *Lucky Catch*. The *Catch* was now at maximum capacity with eight, the added passengers relieved to be out of the bone-chilling water and in the safety of the bigger boat. The younger boy's father wrapped a coat around his son's soggy shoulders, while the older brother reached for some hot chocolate.

I looked around at the floating debris and realized something needed to be done about the tackle boxes and ice chests. Dan volunteered us to stay behind with the capsized dinghy while the Catch took our shivering friends back to the lodge for some steaming hot cocoa and a roaring fire. The captain pushed the throttles down, the bow bucked up high onto plane and the *Lucky Catch* turned and zoomed off.

"Don't forget my RC!" Aaron yelled. I grinned and waved. Everyone waved back as the boat plowed through waves and headed for the mouth of the bay. I could see them shifting around people and blankets, coats, hats, and warm beverages. "Well," I sighed, "that turned out all right." I looked back at all the junk in the water and the overturned dinghy. "What are we going to do with that?"

After cleaning up the floating debris, we found the wind and the chop too dangerous to right the capsized dinghy so we decided to head back to the lodge, leaving the upside down boat floating in the water. "It'll float to shore," Dan reassured us. We planned to come back and pick it up later after the lake had calmed down a little. It was clear Dan wasn't comfortable with the conditions and wasn't ready to risk another mishap. "Leave it." He said definitively.

As we rounded the bend, I could have sworn I saw a hand flop out of the dark, choppy water. I sat straight up in my cold seat and narrowed my eyes as my hand shot out in the direction of what I thought I saw.

"Someone's…someone is swimming out there!" I exclaimed. I instantly regretted what I had said. What kind of ridiculous statement was that? Obviously no one would be swimming in this lake, in these conditions, out in the middle of nowhere with no boat around. Immediately, Dan turned the boat and headed toward where I was pointing.

"Wait, why would anyone be swimming in this weather? I'm sorry. Maybe I'm mistaken." I rubbed my eyes, second-guessing myself, but Dan didn't alter course. His face was solemn. The dinghy beat itself against the oncoming waves. The cold spray flew into our faces and the wind chilled our lips and ears. Miserable weather, miserable it was.

Moments later, to our shock we saw a big man sinking beneath the breakers. The murky water was dragging him down. He looked lifeless. His arms dangled above his head, his hands just beneath the surface. My father and Dan reached down into the water and grabbed him. They grabbed his coat and tried to pull him into the boat, but he was too heavy. We nearly capsized and they had to lower him back into the water. They kept a tight grip on him and held his head out of the water. When the man's face turned up at us, I fell back in shock—it was the captain of the *Lucky Catch*. He was barely alive.

My mind was spinning. *What was the captain doing out here? Where was the boat? Where were the others? Had he fallen overboard?* Dan was much quicker to put two and two together. He stood up and scanned the water then let out a deep and painful moan. As quickly and safely as he could, he steered us to the nearest shore, dragging the captain alongside the boat.

When we reached the pebbled beach, we pulled the man out of the water, turned him on his back and tried to talk to him. His head turned from side to side but he could not speak, suffering from exhaustion and hypothermia. My father and Dan jumped back into the boat and raced out to find more survivors. My brother and I stood silently looking down at the man lying on the beach. He didn't open his eyes, he didn't move and he didn't speak. The realization of what was happening started to creep over me like a dark blanket. Suddenly I was very scared. I prayed a very short prayer, it was all I could muster, *"Oh God please."*

Some time later the men came back empty-handed. Without a word they loaded the captain into the dinghy. He would need medical attention. Dan sped the dinghy, the unconscious captain lying still on the deck, back to the lodge to call for help, leaving my dad, my brother and me alone on shore. A strong wind blew and chilled me to the bone, the waves crashed wildly against the rocks. I looked up at the sky, clouds swirled around high above. The sky offered no comfort. We prayed for our friends, but it was already too late, they were all gone.

Within the hour, a Canadian police boat arrived to pick us up and transport us back to the campground.

By that time, the lake was humming with volunteer patrols. A dozen boats scoured the area, helicopters hovered over the bay, and the rescue divers began to suit up, skillfully preparing their BCDs, checking their regulators and going over dive plans with precision. A glimmer of hope arose in my chest. Surely they would rescue our friends.

The divers looked at me out of the corners of their eyes. They made no such promises. It began to don on me why they weren't in a hurry. This was no longer a rescue. It was a recovery mission.

I stood in the middle of it all, as if invisible, mesmerized by the action. These men were incredibly brave. They weren't afraid of the murky lake water like I was. They were about to go to the bottom of the dark lake and feel around for the lifeless bodies. They were on a mission, volunteering their time to do something horrific so that the families could have closure, ending the agony of worthless hope that maybe somehow, somewhere their loved ones were still alive but simply lost. These courageous divers were going to bring the loved ones home. My admiration for the divers soared. Policemen came and went from our cabin questioning my father and Dan. The professional men and women were instinctively doing what they were trained to do, but they didn't know the victims, these were their jobs. The victims were our friends.

I was born and raised in a third world country. I had never seen anything like this or been up close to real police officers, first responders, or the media, much less this amount of technology and all the unwanted attention. On top of the tragedy and the unimaginable loss, I was more than overwhelmed. I was in shock. I was in a daze. I was living out the longest nightmare of my life.

The adults were inundated with police reports and giving their account of what happened to various agents. My brother and I were the only kids left at camp and seeing that this was a very traumatic experience the men wisely gave us jobs to do to keep us occupied. It was then as I carried the yellow bucket of unused live bait to the edge of the lake to set the minnows free, that the well-meaning volunteer flew his boat up the cement ramp beside me with the first recovered body. The boy who had taken my place on the boat.

That evening we returned to our cabin with heavy hearts and a great sense of loneliness. The camp was quiet once more. The others had all gone home. The four of us—my dad, Dan, my brother and I—were alone in the cabin. Dan called his family from the payphone. When his little girl came to the phone and said "Hi Daddy!" the big farmer lost it. He sobbed and sobbed. It was too hard to watch and I had to walk away. We ate without speaking. The ticking of the clock seemed cruel and loud as darkness settled over us. How I hated how hopeless and helpless I felt.

The next day, the mood was sullen and people plodded on like robots. I was asked to pack up belongings of the other kids who had drowned. I went into their room and sat on Aaron's bed. I looked around at the toys they had left on the floor. I looked at their clothes draped over chairs, socks tossed aside haphazardly, things that reminded me of them. I slowly picked up their things one by one and placed them in a suitcase. God help their mothers when they get these things, I thought. I couldn't begin to fathom their grief. I had only known these kids for a few days and had loved them.

The clock ticked loudly on the wall, its cold hands circled round and round and round. I softly closed the door of the room and we loaded up the van and headed back to our families. After several weeks we got news that all the bodies had been recovered. We learned later that the *Lucky Catch* had gone nose first under a wave and never resurfaced. The freak accident sent the boat straight to the bottom, claiming the lives of four adults and three children.

It was the first time I had stood at the threshold of another world and had seen the door open and close behind the shadows of my friends. I saw the light on the other side disappear, leaving me in darkness once again. I hadn't realized I was in darkness until the door cracked open and I caught a glimpse of that eternal light. Eternity frightened me. I didn't know what happened to a person after they died. I feared what I didn't know or understand.

The night of that horrific tragedy, I had returned to my cabin and saw the boat assignments still taped to the wall. There was my name listed on the registry under *Lucky Catch*. That should have been me in a body bag. I was supposed to be on that boat. Why had I escaped this time? Why had I been left behind? And when would that eternal darkness return to drag me far away from what I knew and loved?

I lay in my bunk and wondered what was behind that mysterious door. What creatures roamed beyond the distant swirling tides of stars and space? Phantoms begged to speak to me while I slept. Still, I couldn't picture the angel of death as a black-hooded skeleton with a sickle. To me he was more like a shark, a soul predator, coming to devour the good and the evil in a seemingly endless rhythm of random tragedies. What unlucky creatures we were to be food for these ghosts. *We're minnows!* I thought in despair.

Confusion and tangled questions tumbled around in my head. I could picture the minnows fleeing back to the deep as I released them from the yellow bucket at the pier of the fish camp. That bucket was simply a container; the life that was inside it, the minnows, had been set free. Just like our friends. But where had they gone? They swam away like the fish into some mysterious place that I didn't know.

I saw the captain of the *Lucky Catch* at his son's memorial service. He was Aaron's father. Dan introduced me, "This is the boy who spotted you that day. He saved your life." Dan put his big calloused hand on my shoulder.

The captain's face hardened and his voice quivered. "You should have left me!" he snarled, with his voice breaking into a cry. "You should have left me!" Then he turned and walked away. I never saw the man again.

During the memorial service, I stared blankly at Aaron's smiling photograph. I imagined him standing on the dock of that wretched lake, popping the top on a can of RC cola, and with a wink and a grin, raising it in a final toast: "Cheers, Bro."

And then he turned, stepped into the water and was gone forever.

> *Have the gates of death been shown to you?*
> *Have you seen the gates of the shadow of death?*
> —God

THE CREATURE

Eighteen months after the tragedy in Canada, our family boarded a plane bound for a long-forsaken part of the world, West Papua. Formerly known as Dutch New Guinea and then Irian Jaya (renamed West Papua in 2007), the large, resource-rich western half of the island was, and remains, a colony of current day Indonesia. My dad was helping to pioneer an International school in Papua with a team of others. Both he and my mom were going to be teachers at the new school.

When we arrived, we stepped off the plane into a little town called Sentani where we were promptly greeted by a warm blanket of moist humidity. Jagged green mountains loomed majestically in front of us and ran down into the sea like scales on the back of a dragon. For me as a teenage boy it would prove to be a place of never-ending mystery and wonder.

I was no stranger to life overseas.

I was born in the Philippines, and apart from infrequent breaks to America, had lived there until age eleven. During those early years of my life, I had seen the faces of sickness, poverty and desperation in the slums and city streets of Manila. In the Philippines I had tasted and seen strange foods like *balut*, a partially developed duck egg. Manila with its concrete jungle, walled houses and squatter settlements, malls and huts emitted the fragrance of jasmine after a refreshing rainstorm that could quickly switch to the smell of sewage on a hot day. I remember eating fresh bread at the neighbor's house, the hospitality of the Filipinos, and playing in their compounds with their children around statues of the Virgin Mary.

For someone of my age, I experienced in the Philippines an unusual myriad of darkness and danger and had become accustomed to happenings that others may have found shocking. I had seen peculiar customs, mystifying behavior, and bizarre traditions involving the black arts and the spirit world. In a land of witch doctors, there were curses, demon possession, and live re-enactments of the crucifixion at Easter.

But nothing had prepared me for what I was about to experience one dark night in our new home in Papua.

I was born into this life and had never known anything different. My grandfather, Dr. Richard S. Pittman, had been in the forefront of pioneering Bible translation to the far corners of the earth, first as a translator himself and then in the capacity as a diplomat and government relations coordinator. My dad had also dedicated his life to improving children's education in remote regions around the globe.

I don't know what age I was when I discovered I wasn't brown. I had always heavily identified with the other local children I grew up with and also with the maids who played a role in raising me. I felt very much Asian, I thought very much like I *was Asian*. My childhood included pig feasts, riding water buffaloes, and walking barefoot around the neighborhood with my friends and our slingshots.

I had a wide variety of unusual pets growing up: a monkey, emerald tree boas, cockatoos, eclectus parrots and lorikeets. Then there were marsupials like wallabies, sugar gliders, cuscuses, and tree kangaroos, to name a few. My favorite was the tree kangaroo because it was cute and fluffy like a little bear and slept in a basket on the couch, but sadly dumb as a doorknob. I wanted so much for it to show a little brain activity but never could get it to do much. And like most marsupials the tree kangaroos were nocturnal so not very fun in the daylight hours.

My dear mother would only allow me to have snakes at home when she wasn't there and didn't know about it and didn't have the opportunity to say no. Unfortunately the boas were always strong enough to lift the lids on the aquarium I kept them in and escaped every night. Once my mom found one of my snakes in the silverware drawer and that was the end of that. I was completely convinced that the reason our house had a bathtub was to keep a crocodile in it but that's where my mom made her stand, something about hell freezing over.

Papua was an entirely different world from what I had known in Manila. I found this forgotten country fascinating. The land was an addictively wild and infinitely intoxicating place, full of dangerous beauty, reeking of adventure around every corner. There were relics and caves that held the leftover stench of the Second World War: abandoned tanks, rusty planes, and all the discarded trash from war; bullets, canteens, helmets, and the odd machine gun. Countless tribes and languages filled the island with beautiful colors, exotic customs and traditions. The land was ancient and enchanting to me.

On one occasion I was trekking over a mountain range and stopped to rest on a ridge when a spry old man with a bow and arrows in his hand scampered up the steep embankment and sat down beside me. We looked each other over unashamedly. He was naked accept for a gourd, the traditional covering for men. I noticed he was covered with battle scars. He noticed my funny clothes and that I smelled of soap.

"You'd never be able to sneak up on anybody, you smell like flowers!" He warned me, wrinkling up his nose in disgust.

"It's the soap." I said, feeling suddenly awkward and suddenly not very manly.

It was quiet for a while but he didn't leave me.

"What a great warrior you must be…" I said. "…to have survived such injuries in battle."

He smiled and looked out over the mountain.

Minutes passed by and he said nothing.

"Tell me about this scar on your face?" I asked, trying to make conversation.

"Oh well… I was shot from a hilltop above. The 6-foot arrow pierced my cheek and went through my chin into my chest and out my back." He said, while reenacting the moment.

"Ouch," I said.

He continued with a laugh, "When I would drink water

it used to come out this hole in my throat!" The memory seemed to really tickle him.

"The arrow went right through?" I enquired.

"Oh no, it got stuck, I had to pull it out myself." He said. He held out one of the arrows he held. "You see this arrowhead, look at the way it's carved. It curves in like this, you can't pull it out, it will rip your guts out. It can only go one way."

I could see the carved hardwood arrow point. It was about a foot long itself with a series of fishhook shaped barbs.

"Oooh... ouch." I grimaced. Realizing this guy was a seriously hard-core warrior, I asked him, "How many people have you killed?"

He sat there silently swaying back and forth on his haunches and then waved his hand over his fingers on one hand and then over his fingers on the other and then over his head. I knew this meant that the number was too great to count.

"How many did you eat?" I said half joking.

"I ate them all," he said, looking me right in the eye.

There was a long uncomfortable silence and then he busted out laughing. I busted out laughing too, I'm not sure why. Sometimes I do that when I'm nervous to ease the tension. So we had a good hard laugh together and then suddenly he stopped and looked me in the eye again quite seriously. I stopped laughing and wondered if he was joking or not.

"Don't worry, I don't do that anymore," he said. "C'mon, let's go."

Before I could process what he just said, he grabbed

me by the hand and helped me the rest of the way up the mountain and then with a look over his shoulder disappeared into the mist.

That was Papua and I loved it and its people. I ran through its lush jungles, was a guest amongst its primitive tribes, and swam in its wild waters. It was beautiful, but there was a distinctive darkness here.

The demonic powers were more noticeable, more real in their elemental nature than anything I had experienced before, even in the Philippines. The people worshiped the spirits of the rocks, trees, animals, and skies. This was a simple and primitive culture; the devil was in no need of disguise. There was no reason to cloak his workings or workers for man's rationalization and scientific dismissal. The dark powers moved freely about here, in a lost garden of trees and men. The devil was bold.

My younger brother, Jeff, and I were housed in a tiny cement guest bungalow with a tin roof that sang beautifully when the rain danced on it. It was the caboose of the house our family was renting in the small town of Sentani. The town was a sleepy little place that had grown up around a World War II airstrip. It lay beneath the shadow of the mighty Cyclops (Mt. Cyclops gets its name from a giant waterfall that springs out of the eye of the 6400-ft. mountain).

Home invasions were rather common in those days so our windows were nailed shut in our quarters and we relied on the small window air conditioner for ventilation. Yet from time to time the bathroom door would fly open for no reason without any breeze to move it. I would glare at the door from my bed, as if scolding it, wishing it not to do that again. The question of who lurked behind our bathroom door made me wonder all the more who lurked behind that mysterious door to the spirit world I feared so much. Out of the corner of my own spirit's eyes, I saw only shadows and questions passing underneath that grand entryway to the afterlife.

On this particular night the air was heavy with moisture and humidity. I retreated to our air-conditioned bedroom hoping that the power wouldn't go off as it frequently had a habit of doing. Being highly introverted, I liked the silence and the cool darkness of our little concrete cocoon. I flopped down into my bed and stared at the ceiling, really not wanting to do my homework.

Suddenly, what appeared to be large human footprints began to cross my ceiling right before my eyes. I could see the outline and the indentation sinking silently as one print appeared after the other and then faded away, as if some invisible man were walking upside down across my room. I closed my eyes and told myself, "That didn't just happen." I forced myself not to peek at the ceiling again for the rest of the night. "I must be so tired I'm seeing things," I rationalized. "Whoo! Maybe I'm a little dehydrated."

I tried to avoid thinking about the possibility of the supernatural being in my bedroom. I had been raised in the Christian faith of my fathers and knew plenty about Jesus and the God of the Bible. I also knew about the pesky fellow in red tights with a pitchfork. He represented nothing more to me than a cartoon character—a fallen angel, too notoriously vain to know a good thing when he had it. I dismissed him as *my enemy*—he was *God's* enemy. God's problem, not my problem. What had I done to get his attention anyway? I was sure there were more important people in the world that he should be interested in. I was just a teen nobody on the far edge of the world. Most of my friends and relatives couldn't even find me on a map. When you're a teenage boy it's hard enough to get the girl you like interested in you... never mind the devil! What would be Lucifer's interest in me? I couldn't imagine, so I didn't.

But he knew right where I was.

It was an ordinary night like any other when I awoke with a start. As my eyes adjusted to the darkness, something felt different; the air was electric. The hair on the back of my neck stood on end. I had a terrible feeling aching in my gut.

Somebody or some*thing* was in the room.

I looked over at my sleeping brother and then at the door. I could tell by the two deadbolts that I religiously checked every night that it was locked. I looked across the bookshelves and closets, scanning every inch of the room, and then I saw it.

The dark visitor hung in the corner by the bathroom door. I had no idea what the creature was, but there it stood before my wide eyes. The figure measured about seven feet tall, yet its feet were not touching the ground. It was floating. I closed my eyes and opened them again, but the specter would not go away. It acknowledged I had seen him by standing to its full height.

It was hovering, it moved up and down like it was breathing as it floated there. It was looking at me, I knew because of the way its head tilted down and then to one side, then to the other. Its form was humanlike, wickedly thin and tall. It had no distinguishable features such as eyes or a nose—not even a face, just an unholy emptiness that held form. I could not see through it; it was a living, breathing darkness.

To my horror, it lunged toward me.

It dashed across the room, turned horizontally over my bed and hovered there. Then it began to smother me.

"O God, what the…!"

My arms were pinned at my sides and I was helpless. I didn't know what to do.

I felt like I was in one of the Sunday school stories I had heard at church, in the storm with Jesus sleeping at the bow of the boat. *Jesus!* I shouted in my mind as if to try and wake him up to rescue me. *Jesus! Jesus! Jesus!*

I was too terrified to speak the words, and Jesus didn't seem like he was going to wake up. I wondered for a second if I had been born into the right religion.

The weight of the thing was pushing me down into my bed. Was it trying to possess my body or kill me? I felt the frame of the bed come up and meet my back through the mattress; it was crushing me.

Jesus! The name gurgled in my throat.

I looked around desperately and saw my brother sound asleep. My mind raced. *Was this really happening to me, or was it a nightmare? My skin felt clammy with sweat. No, this is real!* I pushed back, but it was no use.

Why me, God?! This is so not fair! I haven't… even… done anything!

I couldn't breathe, I was suffocating, the life was being sucked out of me; my soul was being sucked out of me.

The shadowy creature was heavy and thick with death—it was smothering me.

I can't breathe, I can't breathe! I choked. I felt like I was drowning. I felt like I had been holding my breath and now I needed to breathe but I couldn't.

Jesus! Jesus! His name was making its way out of the pit of my stomach to my lips.

"Jesus," I whispered hoarsely. "Jesus, Jesus, Jesus," I said, the whisper growing louder. Somewhere I had heard that speaking the name of Jesus was supposed to work in situations like this. Admittedly, I was a bit inexperienced as a demon fighter, but for some reason I believed it would work instantly. To my dismay it didn't. The creature stopped pushing down on me, but it didn't move, and I still couldn't breathe.

"Jesus, help me!" I gasped. The creature began to pull back. Air seeped into my lungs.

"In the name of Jesus, get off me!" I repeated the phrase over and over. I had no idea what I was doing.

The creature lifted itself off and hovered above me for what seemed an eternity. I was scared out of my mind. Finally, it slowly floated backward to the corner from which it came and gradually evaporated into thin air. My eyes bugged out, I looked again, it was gone. I could feel it was gone.

My lungs were burning like I had been held underwater. My chest burst into life again as I sucked in air.

I leapt out of my bed, grabbed a wooden axe handle, turned on the light and began ransacking the room. Looking under every piece of anything, trying to find a trace of the monster. Sweat streamed down my body and my mind burned red hot with both sheer terror and youthful defiance. If I could find that thing in the light I was going to kill it.

Then I heard a creepy, craggy voice behind me. The hair on the back of my neck stood up again.

"Turn off the light, you idiot. What's the matter with you?" my brother groaned, pressing his pillow over his head.

"Oh it's just you, Jeff!" I let out a sigh of relief.

"Who'd you think it was, Santa Claus? Turn off the light already!"

The door to the other world softly clicked shut as I lay back down again and trembled in a cold sweat.

The next day, I told my dad what had happened. He took me seriously, and summoned the church elders to our house where they prayed that the powers of darkness would leave. I didn't really know what to think about it all. It was the first time I was really forced to think about what I believed about dark powers and such. I could no longer escape the fact that they existed, and for some reason, I was in their crosshairs.

I never saw the creature again, but I heard of others who had encountered something very similar. Years later one of my friends was telling me her daughter was seeing a strange figure appear in her bedroom. She and her husband were having a hard time believing their daughter's claims. I strongly urged them to take her seriously. On further investigation, my friend discovered that these creatures were a familiar presence in West Papua. One of the locals working for them said that these creatures were the original inhabitants of the land. They roamed freely, and were everywhere. The locals could see them and they had always been there, these spirits.

"What do you do when you see them?" The mother had asked.

"We get out of their way," the woman replied.

It was beginning to sink in even deeper to me that there was another world, another dimension and more powerful forces at work in the shadowy universe to be reckoned with.

To be honest, what I really wanted was to mind my own business, and I wanted the universe to leave me alone. I was having a hard enough time making friends with people in the real world, much less having to deal with supernatural conflict. I wasn't prepared for that as a teenager, I didn't think I needed to be. Maybe that was the biggest educational oversight there ever was. It wasn't like math was going to help me survive a demon attack. What was I supposed to do, throw an algebra equation at a monster? And what? Bore it to death? But in all seriousness, I had a lot more questions than answers.

So I lived with the constant turmoil within me, an eternal war between mind and spirit. My mind was telling me to take whatever I could from life to make myself comfortable and happy. My spirit was telling me my life wasn't my own, and that if I didn't take it seriously there would be consequences. It was a war that divided me; all I could think about was finding peace and serenity to still the storm brewing inside. Was I as alone as I felt? Was I in a tug of war for my soul? Was I born of light or of darkness? Where would I end up and why? What was my purpose and what was I supposed to be doing with the relatively few years I was given on this planet? After much restlessness of heart, I determined that if I could not resolve these mysteries with reason and logic, then I would try to escape them.

> *...when I looked for good, evil came; when I looked for*
> *light, then came darkness.*
> —Job

DEEP CALLS TO DEEP

The obsession I had with the mystery of the deep ocean mirrored my obsession to figure out the deep mysteries hidden in my heart. I lay on the beach beneath the West Papuan night sky beside my girlfriend at the time, watching the stars shimmer and enjoying the intimacy that lies within silence and beauty. She pointed to a shooting star, "Look! Make a wish."

I smiled. "God's painting shells and throwing them into the sea."

"Is that right?" Her eyes sparkled with humor as she turned to look at me.

"Yeah, well…that's what I'm going to tell my kids someday."

She put her hand on my chest and played with the broken shells on my necklace. The edges of her lips wrinkled as she pretended to be serious, "People will think your kids are crazy!" She laughed.

I raised my eyebrows in amusement. "Maybe only crazy people are happy." I wanted to be happy, like I was right then. I wanted to be in that moment forever. I felt like my whole life I was looking to belong, to know someone and be known. To be loved for me, for who I was, in spite of myself.

The life we lived overseas, it was good sometimes, and it was hard sometimes. People came and went. You would get close to someone and they would have to move. We said a lot of goodbyes. My heart was broken and full of grief most of the time.

But whenever I was able to make a special connection with someone, part of that relationship we shared was with the ocean.

I was so comfortable by the sea, anything I wanted to say could be spoken there in the beauty of these kind of Edenic moments, just me, the girl and the sea. If ever I couldn't find the words I wanted to say, the sea would find them for me. The way the sun lights the eye, and also gives it shadows. The way the waves thunder grandly and leave you deaf to the whispers of the wind. The way the body gives heat and it is quickly stolen from you. If someone could love the paradox of those moments with me, then they could love me.

I felt the same burden of enigma in myself, that constant war between the limitations of my physical world and my seemingly infinite spirit, between reason and faith.

The Pacific Ocean surrounding Papua holds a beauty and mystery all its own. Growing up, I loved to spend countless hours exploring its reefs and lagoons. Magnificent coral colonies rivaled any architectural achievements I had ever seen. The reef fish were more abundant and colorful than a handful of rainbows. I swam beside enormous bump-headed wrasse the size of a door, along with green, purple, blue and yellow parrotfish, moorish idols, imperial angelfish, sharks, rays, butterfly fish, lion fish and every strange shape and color of sea creature one could imagine—from puffers to nudibranchs. My thirsty eyes could not get enough of the ocean's marvels, its living kaleidoscope of life. I was in constant awe of the mysteries of the deep. These were mysteries of a world I was keen to explore, unlike the spiritual enigmas that I feared beyond the eternal door.

I could relate to her, the sea, though I could not understand her. After all, she was like the war inside me, full of life and full of death at the same time. No one could know the mysteries of the depths of my heart: neither the great joys nor the great pain, the tides of aching to live for something extraordinary, to grow greater than the shell of doubt and fear that confined me, and to break the chains of loneliness that bound me. All those I loved, I wanted to come and sit with me beside the ocean's waters. To experience what I felt. To be silent and hear my heart in the pulsing of her waves, and to simply appreciate and respect something that can't always be understood.

I liked to dive down into the clear blue water to see how deep I could swim. I heard that there were free divers who could descend to unbelievable depths on one breath of air. I wanted to be like them, to have that freedom to disappear into the peaceful netherworld. No one could bother me there; it was quiet, serene, only the soft ticking and clicking of sea creatures could be heard. Surely here amongst the coral and its inhabitants, like sunken treasure, must lay the peace I sought.

Marawai was the local boat captain who brought me to those remote beaches, since there were no roads to them.

He wore a tattered baseball cap, an old shirt and shorts; his humble appearance and demeanor would cause most people to overlook the man. Lines of wisdom and experience lined his face the way only a life on the sea brings, along with a mischievous twinkle in his eye. He had been a motorcycle courier for the Allies in WWII on his island. The more I got to know him, the more I marveled at what an incredible life he had lived.

I asked Marawai once, "What is the most unusual thing you have ever seen in your years on the ocean?"

He thought long and said, "Whales, as far as the eye could see." I often try to imagine what that incredible day must have been like.

In spite of the tragedy I had experienced in Canada, I still loved being in the boat on the sea. Marawai's boat was narrow, about 18-feet long, made of wood with long bamboo outriggers and an unreliable outboard motor. I would drift contentedly for hours with him when the engine would putter out. It never really bothered me too much; I trusted him and genuinely enjoyed being with him. He would take out a spark plug, blow on it, sand it a little, put it back and pull the cord. When it wouldn't start, he'd patiently do it all over again. I didn't know anything about engines, so I would watch and ask the occasional question.

I had been in rough seas with Marawai more than once. The worse the weather the brighter the twinkle in his eye, and if he was standing… well if he was standing we were in for a fight with the sea. And I could swear he loved it. I felt safe with Marawai. He was born with saltwater in his veins and you could sense the connection between him and the sea.

I had seen that wink and smile a number of times. The most memorable was one stormy night when we were heading out to a spot we called "the outside beach" because it was outside the relative protection of the bay. It was about midnight and although the waves were high on the open sea, they still had a way of rocking me to sleep. Suddenly, I awoke, feeling like we were airborne. The boat was creaking and rolling from side to side, someone was bailing water, and the sea was drenching us from all sides. I looked around for white caps to see how high the waves were. Two stories over us on the starboard side, I saw the crest of the wave we had just fallen from.

I looked back at Marawai to see his reaction. There is a saying among seafarers, "You don't have to worry until the captain's worried." Marawai just winked and smiled.

Marawai used to call me *Penjaga Pantai*, the "Guardian of the Beach." He'd say with a smile, "It should be your job to stay here and watch over things."

"Yes it should," I'd reply, "Yes it should."

He'd laugh. He knew how much I loved the ocean. We had come from different worlds but we had our love for the sea in common. I felt like a fish out of water at school. I was bored in class and struggled socially, being as introverted as I was. The beach was the perfect place for me. It was one of the few places where I didn't feel stressed. In fact I was genuinely happy there. I couldn't get back to it fast enough.

Sometimes I imagined there was some kind of cosmic mistake, that I was meant to have gills and didn't. I thought of the ocean day and night. I wanted to be in it, on it, around it. I loved the beach, the sunsets, the sunrises. Watching turtles come up to lay their eggs at night, the full moon on the water, dolphins playing. The way the colors changed, I likened my emotions to its kaleidoscope of blues and greens. The sea was like the many shades of wisdom. To covet being taught by her, to listen silently to her changing moods, to wonder at her depths, her beauty and her danger fed my obsession to be with her.

I loved her and I feared her all at once. I wrote her poetry and cursed her. The thing that gave joy to my life would just as soon kill me… I knew that very well but she consumed me. I lost myself to her wooing. My only relationships that withstood this affair were with those who accepted this mystery and its power over me. The rest were broken by my desire to escape any heartache or pain by running to the caress of her waves. Ironically, I went to her because I was lonely; I went to her because she was lonely. I knew that she would take me in every time but still she left me wanting. Wanting to go deeper, wanting to see more, wanting to experience something that had not thrilled me before, wanting to discover and wanting to feel whole and alive. Deeper mysteries than those of the sea ached in my soul to be explored.

The thing about the ocean is that the deeper one dives, the darker it becomes. Such was becoming the journey of my life.

…the sea, once it casts its spell, holds one in its net of wonders forever.
—Jacques Yves Cousteau

Have you journeyed to the springs of the sea
or walked in the recesses of the deep?
—God

Deep calls to deep...all your waves and breakers have
swept over me.
—Psalmist

SOMEONE IS TRYING TO KILL ME

The pilot told us it wasn't going to be a full flight. There were to be fourteen passengers on board the Indonesian plane. My friend Uncle Wally and I eagerly accepted the invitation to take a free exploratory trip on a local airliner from West Papua to Lombok, an island near Bali.

Uncle Wally was the head carpenter at one of the missionary bases in Sentani, and would later become the director. We became friends one summer when I volunteered to work for him. In the little community where we lived, it was not uncommon to give the title "Uncle" and "Aunt" to the adults we interacted with weekly. After all, most of us knew them better than our own extended families who were so far away. Through the course of many adventures together, Uncle Wally and his family had a profound influence in my life. Uncle Wally and I looked forward to every opportunity to explore the ocean around the province of West Papua and the entire island nation of Indonesia. It is rare to find someone with the natural ability to find eternal meaning in the beauty of the islands and the amazing experiences shared together.

No story is complete or satisfactory without a character who is an anchor of wisdom and guidance. At home, I was fortunate to have this in my father. Outside of that, I was blessed to have the friendship of Uncle Wally and his family. I had a tendency to question everything and he had concise and true answers for me. What he didn't know, we would seek the answers for together. I came to greatly appreciate his humility, genuineness, honesty and confidence in me.

Clearly he saw something in me that I couldn't see myself.

The more I tried to understand who I was and what my purpose was on this planet, the more I discovered it wasn't at all about me. I was once under the impression, as a young person, that I was the lead actor in the play of life. I thought primarily along the lines of what benefited me and what didn't. I saw the world as my personal oyster shell. I didn't realize how selfish I was, that life was not primarily about me but about how I (and indeed all of us) fit into a higher plan and purpose.

When the day of the exploration flight arrived, Uncle Wally was sick in bed after contracting malaria. It was pretty normal for us to get malaria in Papua. We got it like most people get a cold. Although there were times when it could be quite serious. I was with Uncle Wally at his house when the Indonesian pilot came by to see if we'd be going along on the exploratory flight. He told me I was still welcome to come along even though Uncle Wally wasn't able to go, which I thought was a nice gesture. I knew it was a rare adventure opportunity to fly over to Lombok, but decided I would rather not go without Uncle Wally. The pilot waved goodbye with a smile.

That was the last time we saw him. The following day we heard the plane had vanished. Soon we learned it had crashed into a mountain on Lombok, with no survivors.

When the pilot's body was returned to his family, Uncle Wally and I went to pay our respects. The pilot's coffin sat in the center of the room. The body already smelled bad since it had been nearly a week in the jungle before it was recovered. Every fifteen minutes or so someone would come in and spray it with half a can of Lysol. On top of the coffin sat a picture of the pilot, looking alive and happy. I couldn't help but feel uncomfortable at the irony of that cheery picture sitting on top of his corpse.

Years later I would have the opportunity to stay with a North American Indian tribe and they had a custom of taking pictures with their dead loved ones, pictures taken of the body with the whole family. That made even less sense to me at the time, but now even snapshots with corpses felt more realistic than this. At least one could have a sense of closure with such a photo and know the person was gone. I squirmed in my chair as I watched the kids play happily around the coffin, as if not fully understanding that their dead father was lying inside.

It struck me then in the midst of that bustling home, that life goes on without you. This man's kids would grow up, marry, get jobs, have kids, and this place would eventually remember him no more. The airlines would surely get a new pilot; his wife may even remarry. Confusion about the transience and meaning of life mingled in my head like the smell of death and flowers in the room.

Here was death again, so much death. Where was the final destination for the soul? What was the purpose of it all? Who would miss me if I were to die? I couldn't really think of any reason why anyone would miss me for very long. Where was my life headed anyway? How long did I have? And what was I going to do with that time? Who was in control? It was clear that I wasn't and I certainly had more questions than answers. The ocean made me feel small and helpless; death made me feel even more helpless. Even in the prime of my life, even in the midst of the deceptive invincibility of youth I was humbled into submission by thoughts of death and decay.

These interrogations haunted me like restless ghosts. Our dead friend's photo seemed to be looking right at me, daring me to answer these questions. His kids were laughing and playing nearby, fluids from the corpse were leaking through the makeshift plywood coffin, the room smelled of death, the woman with the Lysol reappeared and doused the room in a cloud of chemical fragrance... I sipped my lemon juice nervously... these were all things I didn't want to think about. These things made me feel old inside.

My scrapes with death didn't slow down; they increased, provoking even more confusion in me as to my future. One rainy night I was driving home on the road that wound around the lake from Abepura to Sentani, about a thirty-minute drive. Torrential rain poured down around me in sheets. The lights of my motorcycle reflected back in my eyes, as if the wall of water was a mirror.

Suddenly, out of the cold misery of the night, a gravel truck came barreling around the corner behind me and hit me. I was thrown off the motorcycle and hydroplaned about 30 feet down the road into the oncoming lane. The truck continued on without braking, disappearing into the night.

When I stopped sliding, I gingerly lifted myself off the road. Shaking, I stood in the center of the road and looked myself over. I found not one scratch. "Huh," I mused.

The motorcycle, on the other hand, had not been so lucky. As I pulled the bike from the embankment that sloped down to the lake, I wondered how I had survived that accident. All the glass on the bike had been broken, the fenders were snapped, and anything that had been sticking out was now sticking in. I found a rock and beat the foot pegs and brake-peddle back down. I beat the handlebars back out and jimmy-rigged a few things together. The motor started after several kicks and I managed to limp the bike back to my house.

Nobody was home and the door was locked, so I dropped the motorcycle in the front yard and walked over to the dormitory for a hot shower. When my parents came home and saw the wreckage in the lawn they feared I was dead. They were relieved to find out I was just next door having hot cocoa.

On another occasion, I was alone, climbing up a cliff at a remote beach. Wearing only a pair of surf shorts, I had been exploring and was trying to get around the cliffs to another beach. Somehow, I'd climbed quite high and found myself in a precarious situation. I couldn't go back the way I came, but I couldn't reach across to the next hold safely.

Eventually, I had to lunge for a handhold. I caught the rock, but it came loose and I began to fall backward, passing the point of no return. Suddenly I felt the distinct pressure of a hand on my back, pushing me up against the rock face. I looked behind me and saw only sky. *Weird*, I thought to myself.

Not long after, as I was riding my motorcycle to Uncle Wally's house, a van pulled out in front of me and stalled, completely blocking off the street. I stood up and put all of my weight on the brake peddle, but it was no use. I was going to hit the van fast and hard. Suddenly, my back tire locked up, throwing the bike out of control and onto the side path. People were yelling and jumping out of the way. I slid into a makeshift *warung* (food stall) that someone was setting up with poles and sheets, and made it out to the other side. The wheel unlocked, the bike popped back up on the other side of the van, righted itself and I was on my way. I looked over my shoulder in disbelief at what had just happened. The van was still stalled in the road, and the crowd went back to their business, but I was alive.

When I reached Uncle Wally's place, his wife Joan said, "You look like you've seen a ghost! Are you all right?"

"Yeah," I said, pausing while I watched my hands shake. There was a long silence, and then I continued. "This might sound weird, but it feels like someone or something is trying to kill me…. and I can't die."

She set a cold soda in front of me and said, "Maybe God has a reason he wants you around."

I couldn't get those words out of my head. Why would God want me around? Of what possible use could I be to him? I wasn't even living for him. I was living for myself. I simply couldn't imagine. At the rate I was going, I would be lucky to reach twenty. But thoughts of death and eternity freaked me out. If I was going to find out what God's plan was, I was going to have to ask him. If I was going to ask him, I was going to have to get to know him.

But that could wait…or so I thought.

> *What is the way to the abode of light?*
> *And where does darkness reside?*
> *Can you take them to their places?*
> *Do you know the paths to their dwellings?*
> —God

CROCODILES ARE GOOD LISTENERS

Every school kid, no matter what age, looks forward to summer vacation. I was no different, but summers were lonely for me in West Papua. That was the time of year all my friends cleared out of town and went back to their village homes, Europe, Australia, or America. Sometimes it seemed as if my family and I were the only ones left on the coast.

I decided before my junior year of high school that I was going to be proactive and make my own summer fun. I hated being lonely, I felt like I lived most of my life in a tiny cave in my own head. I was tired of listening to my own voice, and I was tired of feeling like I had no direction or purpose in life. Verbally I acknowledged God and a higher purpose to life, but the truth of the matter was that it didn't mean much to me at the time.

I needed another adventure, another escape. That was my mantra. I looked for escape in the ocean, in relationships, in adventure, anywhere and in any way to try and get away from the insecurity and loneliness I felt in my own heart. To get away from the nagging questions that haunted me.

To drown out my conscience and the pull I was beginning to feel on my heart from somewhere I did not yet know or understand.

I'd been wanting a windsurf board for a while, so I asked my dad if he could get me one in Singapore or Jakarta. He looked around, but they were expensive and difficult to ship to our island. I hadn't given up, though, and I kept pestering my dad about it. He said, "Why don't you ask God for one?"

So I did. Partly out of frustration and partly out of sarcasm. "God, can I have a windsurf board?" It was a ridiculous request. I didn't know God very well and God certainly didn't owe me anything. But it wasn't like I had any other options either.

Not long after that, a Dutch sailor sailed into the bay. The sailor said, "Hey, I've got this windsurf board cluttering up my deck, do you know of anyone who would want one?" So that's how I got my first windsurf board, from the Dutch sailor and my sarcastic prayer.

With the help of a pilot friend, Paul Westlund, we managed to get my board into a Helio courier (a single prop airplane) and fly it out to Lake Holmes. Helios were slow and loud but they could land anywhere and carry a lot of weight. Flying in one was like pushing an old lawnmower slowly through the sky. Paul was enthusiastic and larger than life. He had a lot of energy and was a go-to guy if you had a crazy idea. He served faithfully for many years as a much loved pilot in West Papua and would one day pay the ultimate price, losing his life in an airplane accident doing what he loved, furthering the gospel through Bible translation by helping missionaries reach the remotest areas by bush plane.

At that time, Lake Holmes, or *Danau Bira*, was a large mission outpost in the jungle, built on one side of the lake. The outpost served as sort of a central base and jump off point to more remote tribes that the missionaries were serving even farther interior. My grandfather had opened this mission outpost a couple decades before I ever set foot there. Wooden houses were spread along the lake connected by a raised wooden boardwalk with hibiscus and plumeria trees interspersed quaintly among the jungle homes. The first time I saw it, I immediately fell in love with the place.

I talked my parents into letting me spend the summer at Lake Holmes with some friends who were doing translation in the area. The friends eventually left but I remained at the outpost by myself. I'd brought a couple boxes of food with me on the plane that held me over until nearby residents started to feel sorry for me and invited me over for meals.

The local people near Lake Holmes had long been peaceful and some had converted to Christianity due to the large missionary presence there.

I didn't taste a hint of any of the dangers that had sadly happened to others in remote parts of the country. In 1968 two missionaries, Phil Masters and Stan Dale, crossed over a ridge where the people on the other side thought they were spirit creatures. The frightened mountain people chased the missionaries, killed them with bows and arrows and scattered their mutilated body parts throughout the jungle.

A friend of mine who grew up with the Yali tribe told me recently that the natives may have realized the guys weren't spirit creatures by the time they killed them. But they certainly feared Stan, who seemed unkillable. They thought he surely had supernatural power. Afraid this "gospel" would change them and weaken the power of their witch doctors and traditional leaders, they acted in fear of repercussions from the spirit world. I can understand that. I was a little bit afraid of the spirit world myself.

Phil Master's wife continued on as a single missionary there in a place called Karubaga, where I had the opportunity to meet her years later. The mountains where that tragedy took place were far from my summer retreat at Lake Holmes, and I felt safe among the local people.

I was supposed to work for an old guy who wanted me to cut up a rusty WWII generator and dump it in the middle of the lake but after about the fifth hacksaw blade broke and I hadn't even scratched it, I opted out of that work opportunity. I never had the patience for pointless busy work. I had more important things to do, like wind surf and explore.

I was sort of convinced by this time in my youthful ignorance, and from what I had already survived, that I was somewhat invincible, so the fact that Lake Holmes had crocodiles in it thrilled me. The wind was excellent and I had a great time sailing every day. Hornbills and cockatoos flew overhead, sounding like prehistoric creatures with their screeching and large wings swooshing through the air. Giant trees loomed on the banks and large floating islands made up of some kind of water plants that had attracted a variety of flora over the years drifted with the wind. Every day when I set sail I found the lake was pristine and vacant except for the occasional fisherman in a dugout canoe, me and the elusive crocodiles. It was peaceful.

I kept my board and sail in a nearby shed. Early in the

morning and at sunset I would haul it out, slide it into the water, pop the sail into the universal joint on the deck, step lightly onto the board, pull the boom gently around till wind filled the sail and off I'd go silently across the lake. In the morning a light fog often settled on the water and I would glide through it like I was sailing through the clouds.

One particular day I sailed to the very far corner of the lake and followed a little inlet. I noticed a small trail leading into the jungle and curiosity got the best of me. I found some cassowary tracks (a large flightless bird, like an emu) and followed them. (Ironically, many years later, I was watching a National Geographic special where an explorer set off down the very same trail. He claimed he was the first man to ever explore that area. I shook my head and rolled my eyes at the TV.)

With my eyes glued to the cassowary tracks, I noticed some other tracks in the mud as well. Were these tree kangaroos, I wondered? Maybe I would come across one of these animals if I was lucky. Crouching down so I could see the tracks better, I continued down the trail quietly. Suddenly feeling that I was not alone, I looked up and startled a group of soldiers heading toward me. It took me a minute to figure it out, but these soldiers were government soldiers. That's the first important thing to discern in most countries: the government soldiers as opposed to rebel forces.

Indonesia invaded Papua in 1961 and, according to historians, handpicked elders who would agree to remain under Indonesian rule. The indigenous people of West Papua have a history of resisting colonization and their desire for independence has been a continuing point of conflict. The government stationed soldiers in strategic locations to discourage the outbreak of rebellious indigenous groups. When you come across guys in the jungle holding guns, you always want to know what their politics are.

Immediately obvious was the fact that they were pretty far from headquarters, or hadn't had an inspection in awhile. Their uniforms were in disarray, they were unshaven and they had different colored bandanas tied around their heads and arms. I took this to mean that there was somewhat of a lack of accountability. They were heavily armed and suddenly seemed agitated by the shoeless, shirtless white kid in surf shorts.

The leader of the group squared up to me as the others circled behind. He stuck the barrel of his automatic rifle up my right nostril and asked me in Indonesian,

"Who are you, and what do you think you're doing out here?"

I assumed he was being sarcastic and didn't really care who I was, but the cold steel in my nostril told me I had better think of a good answer quickly. I was thinking that I probably should have told someone where I was going before I left that morning. Nobody in the whole wide world knew where I was. That was a pretty common theme for me from the time I was a little kid, but on this day I wish I had told someone.

I took a deep breath and forced a smile as I gingerly plucked the gun barrel out of my nose, "Uh, hehe, funny story...I was looking for you guys."

They looked at each other, confused.

"How did you know where we were?" he demanded.

"Why were you looking for us?" the soldier barked.

I looked at my bare feet for a while, I looked at their muddy boots, I looked at a tree with thorny bark, stalling while I desperately searched my mind for a good response to free me from a potential disaster. They were waiting for an answer.

"Oh…well…uh…I heard you guys like to play volleyball."

If there's one thing I knew about Indonesian soldiers, it's that they love to play volleyball.

They lowered their guns and the young man behind me blurted out, "We DO like to play volleyball!"

Another one said, "We've got a game this afternoon!"

The leader glared at his men who seemed to have forgotten their place, and then glared back at me. After a long silence, he tapped me on the chest with his gun and asked with a smirk, "Well, are you going to come play with us or not?"

I accompanied them back to their jungle outpost, comprised of five or six makeshift huts in a muddy clearing. From the looks of the simple camp it looked like these guys had been there awhile. No wonder they were bored, there's not a lot of entertainment options in the jungle. Especially if it's foreign to you as it would have been for these city boys. By the time we sat down, the soldiers were much more relaxed and had dropped the tough guy act and were very pleasant to me. I no longer felt threatened and realized most of them weren't much older than I was.

I ended up playing volleyball there nearly every day until I left Lake Holmes at the end of the summer. I came and went as I pleased and even made a few friends. I didn't ask them about their mission or why they were there; it was obvious like most soldiers they were following orders and putting in their time. I had learned early on to stay out of local politics and mind my own business. It was never appreciated when foreigners stuck their noses where they didn't belong.

One afternoon I was sitting in the shade of a breadfruit tree with them, watching a bored soldier feed batteries to a young cassowary. I glanced over at their commander, who raised his eyebrows with an amused grin, acknowledging me. I started thinking about what he had asked me that first day on the cassowary trail, "Who are you?"

I hadn't ever really answered that. It was an important question. I didn't have a title, and I didn't have much of what I'd call an identity. I had an American passport but was born and raised in Asia. I looked white and felt brown. I had a family and friends but still felt alone, especially here in the jungle with strangers and Indonesian soldiers. There was nothing to identify me but a windsurf board and some volleyball skills. I was alive but felt dead.

Was that it? Was I simply an adventure junkie and an athlete? In a way, that was the identity I had come to accept—in a way, it was how other people saw me. That identity seemed as lonely as my summer vacations. I looked at the cassowary gulping down the battery. Locals would take a cassowary egg that was bigger than a softball and blow the yoke out through a small hole. Once empty they would carve an incredible picture on the outside of it and sell it to tourists. I felt hollow like that. Hollow… with a cliché little picture stamped on me. Now all I had to do, according to the world we live in, was spend the rest of my life trying to get people to see value in that. I sighed.

At sunset, I meandered down to the dock alone sucking the nectar out of some pretty orange flower. The jungle was abuzz at that time with the sounds of a million hungry insects. I watched the full moon climb into the sky like a giant volleyball.

Tossing a stone into the dark water, I complained to the crocodiles. "I'm not just an empty egg shell." They didn't say anything, they just listened. Crocodiles are good listeners.

RAPTURE DAYS

The stars lit up the sky like diamonds spilled across a dark blanket, making it shimmer with life. They looked so small, but shone so brightly, giving the night a warm velvety-blue color, like the inside of a jewelry box. I drove my motorcycle through a field of tall elephant grass to a secluded cement slab on a hill overlooking the town. The slab was a remnant from a WWII US army outpost. I put down the kickstand, dismounted and rolled onto my back.

I came here often to think. I breathed in the cool evening air and listened to the wind rustle through the grass. I was a constant pilgrim in search of serenity and I found a slice of it here. The grass seemed to filter out any noise but the sounds of nature, like a whale uses baleen to filter krill. I stared at the stars so intently I saw through the first luminous layer, deep into the Milky Way…I was awestruck.

For a moment I thought seriously about stars, planets and the science of the solar system. In my mind's eye I could see my science teacher pointing to colored Styrofoam balls, trying to make the complexities of the universe sound simple so we could be quizzed on them. I marveled at all the detailed "systems" in nature. We learned in science that a system is an organized set of interconnected complex parts that work together to make a whole. Systems are not random at all, they are clearly designed to work a certain way all the time, and in nature they do. So who designed these systems? Especially the unfathomable complexity of the human body systems, and the solar system, and the incredibly diverse eco-systems all around me. I could not accept that it was possible that any of these systems randomly evolved; that would require more faith than to believe they were designed by a higher power.

I was spellbound by the changing colors within each star, swirling balls of cosmic gas. They really did look like diamonds, these gleaming prisms of light. I reached up as if to pluck one from the sky. I smiled, "If only…"

The grass bent over with the wind into my private sanctuary, my simple cathedral. The smile left my face and my eyebrows furrowed. What was out there? Other worlds? Other people? God? Satan? Swirling balls of cosmic gas?

A book had been circulating at my high school about the Rapture—that long anticipated prophesy of when Jesus Christ would return in the sky, the trumpet of the angel Gabriel would sound, and those who believed in the Messiah and his resurrection would ascend to meet him in the sky to be taken to heaven. The author claimed his calculations had revealed the rapture would be happening sometime that very week. I thought it was pretty gutsy to put all your credibility on the line to make a bold prediction like that and publish it.

I didn't pay much attention to it at first, but as my family talked about it around the table and my friends discussed it at school, I started to wonder if it might be true. There was a lot of evidence given in that book as to the author's reasons for his prediction, and it all sounded quite credible. Some who had read it thought he was crazy and others thought him a prophet. I didn't know. I don't mean to be sacrilegious but it occurred to me that the line between crazy and prophet was often pretty blurry.

Needless to say, there was much discussion about the rapture that week. I was actually quite curious about how this was all supposed to work out in reality. At school, someone boldly stated we would disappear when the trumpet sounded, and our clothes would be piled up on the floor. Another said we would float up into the sky to meet Jesus. I wondered what that would be like... flying up through the universe stark naked with my classmates and millions of strangers. My only comfort came when the Bible teacher said we wouldn't be able to take our eyes off Jesus. I thought that was good, if we were all going to be naked.

One discussion determined that when we were "taken" there would be terrible accidents, airplanes would crash, cars would collide, and I could be whisked off my motorcycle in the middle of the road. I glared at my bike, "Figures, I just got you all fixed up. The only time you decide to run is when I'm going to be taken up to heaven."

I looked back at the stars as if looking into the eyes of God. "You're coming for me too, right?" Why was I uncertain? I didn't know my Bible well enough. "If I get left behind, the first thing I'm going to do is read my Bible more." I lamented the fact that I had waited so long to read something so critical to my life.

I wearily stood up and saddled the old motorcycle and switched the key on. I gazed once more at the sky, gave the engine a good kick and the motorcycle leapt to life. I shook my head and rolled my eyes.

I wheeled her back to the path and followed the winding trail back to the road, headed for home.

When I walked in, I heard my family talking intensely about the rapture. My mom said she was going to get out the stash of candy she had been saving all year and we were going to eat it all. Just in case. I sat down and started munching on the prized American chocolate that was so hard to come by in Indonesia at the time.

My dad turned off the generator that ran our electricity and we sat together in the living room, our faces illuminated by candles. I looked around the room at my family and felt thankful for them. I wondered if we would still be a family in heaven. There was so much I didn't understand about eternity. Was it really on our doorstep? I felt anxious and afraid.

The author of the rapture book claimed the rapture would take place on one of three days during that week. When the first day came around, we all joked about it at school, nervously. My friend confided in me that he was wearing his clean underwear.

One wise guy asked the teacher, "Since we are going to be raptured, do we have to do our homework?" I thought that was a fair question.

The teacher smiled, "If you're raptured, your homework isn't due, but if you're left behind it is."

I wondered what was the point of having classes if we were going to be taken up to heaven. I suggested we just have a half-day of school. We never got snow days in the tropics, we could at least have rapture days.

The first day came and went, and none of us were raptured. If anyone was they were sent back, because the next day everyone was present and accounted for.

During the second day of the prophecy, I noticed people were treating each other with a greater love and respect. Some were dressed nicer, and even the school troublemakers behaved respectfully. I remembered there was someone I had treated unkindly. I found her and apologized, she was very gracious and forgiving. Anything I thought of that needed to be made right, I attempted to correct. I saw others doing likewise. The joking about the rapture subsided, and people seemed to be thinking more carefully about their actions, about their lives.

That evening, our family sat around the candles again. My dad read from Scripture about the rapture. I liked being together as a family. The second day came and went with no trumpet sound.

On the final day of the prophecy, people became very serious. Some, I might say, were even sweating it out. I was one of them. Those three days of school were the most peaceful and unified days the student body had ever experienced! When you're thinking about the imminent return of Jesus and standing before him to give account of your actions, it does something to your behavior. You start thinking about the way you are acting, treating people and speaking to one another. There was an abundance of love and selflessness that week.

The daylight hours passed by in a blink and soon it was

night. The stars were the clearest I had ever seen them. My dad was returning from shutting off the generator. I could hear his footsteps approaching, crunching on the gravel road. How strange and ghostly quiet that night was.

I was starting to worry. "Don't leave me behind, God. No... please don't forget me here—if you do come, that is."

I began to feel nervous. I wondered if Jesus was nervous. I wondered if he was adjusting his robe, and double checking the protocol, lining the angels up and inspecting the ranks. "Gabriel! Do you have the trumpet? Fine! Did you test it out? Have you practiced your notes? Splendid! All set then? Right, follow me, everyone!"

What was I going to say? "Hi, um, here's a few reasons why I should get to go to heaven...." No, that wasn't right. I tossed and turned in my bed, then looked up at the ceiling fan. The power had been switched off but I had wondered earlier if you were raptured through a ceiling fan, how you'd turn out. *I should be thinking more serious thoughts.* My mental rehearsal of the holy rapture was turning out to be more like a Monty Python skit. Jesus was going to be disappointed with me, I was sure of it.

Then suddenly, loud and sharp, a trumpet blast shattered the stillness of the night and I sat upright in my bed.

Wild eyed with consternation, my heart felt like it imploded and sank to the bottom of my stomach. I was not being elevated into the air. In fact my body felt as heavy as my heart. I was going to be left behind!

"Why God? Why?!" I started to tug at my hair in agony, when I thought, hold on, maybe Jesus was going to wait until the end of the song.

I cocked my head and listened more carefully to the melody; maybe I should be humming along. What is the procedure? I should have paid more attention in Sunday school. I'm sorry to say, Gabriel's trumpet solo, it was terrible. Gabriel couldn't carry a tune. He had not been practicing. They were going to need a do over. Jesus was going to have to go back and get another trumpet player. You know, you'd think for such an important occasion that we'd all waited a couple thousand years for, they could get that...wait a second! I sprung from my bed and shouted, "Hey! Who's out there?"

From the next bedroom over, my brother let out a cry of relief, "Ray! I knew you'd still be here."

"Yeah, yeah." I threw open my door and ran down the hall. "Wait, what?" I didn't have time to argue with my brother right now about the fact he was still here too.

My dad shouted, "If that's Gabriel, it's the worst trumpet playing I've ever heard!"

The whole family, pajama clad, dashed down the hall and out the front door. I wasn't sure what my plan was yet, it was either to leap up and grab Gabriel by the heel and hitch a ride or full on body tackle him for screwing up the rapture song. In the front yard we discovered a group of our more mischievous friends rolling on the ground belly laughing, two of them clutching old trumpets. The Papuan night watchman looked on, holding his longbow and arrows, utterly confused by our game.

One of our friends, holding his sides, exclaimed with tears in his eyes, "We've been here awhile, but we had to find the night watchman and tell him not to shoot us!" The group doubled over in raucous laughter again.

"You know what?" we said to the watchman, "Go ahead and shoot them."

~ ~ ~ ~ ~

So as it turned out, I wasn't raptured. I'm still here on planet Earth and we decided not to murder our friends after all. But it might have been a close call for me, it was one of many second chances. I'm not sure I would have made the cut. I'm not sure God could say he knew me.

Growing up around Christians my whole life, I guess I never really had a clear sense of what it was like to be truly lost.

Years later when I was in my 20s I would end up volunteering for a search and rescue team that worked for the sheriff's department in a small town in rural USA. One of the training programs we had to do was to be tested in a cave rescue scenario. This involved taking us all deep underground during the winter and putting us through a variety of tight spaces and challenging scenarios to see if any of us would crack. It concluded with us having to swim through an underwater tunnel out of the cavern through a small hole. The last thing you want in a cave rescue is to have to rescue one of the rescuers, so we were pushed to see how far we could be pushed.

I didn't have any issues with the cave environment. I wasn't anxious or bothered by the tight spaces or the darkness. There were about a dozen of us and we were all following a couple firemen, highly experienced cavers who had a map of this particular cave system. In fact there were so many of us with headlamps on, it occurred to me bringing up the rear that I didn't really even need to have my light on. So to save batteries I shut it off and just relied on the light from the others. I used up their light and their energy.

That pretty much summed up my life with Christians to that point. I followed behind at a distance without a light of my own, I used the light that flooded from others to find my way. But it wasn't the same as having my own light, I could see only dimly and not very far. I was trusting that whoever was in the front knew where they were going. It doesn't seem like you're lost when you're following people who know where they are going. But I wasn't committed to their path, and I wasn't on a path of my own because I didn't know where I was going.

It probably wasn't until we took a break after being in the cave for four or five hours that one of the lead firemen noticed.

"Hey, you don't have a light!"

"I don't need one, you know where you're going and all these other people have a light."

"When all our batteries die, we'll end up following you!" he joked.

That was a scary thought.

But we weren't lost and all I had to do was play along and I knew how to do that. I had been playing that game my whole life. And the darkness? Well I had known the darkness very well. I could make a home in it. That's what I thought, but the reality was I always had a way out. I always had a back up, or back door, or someone in my life who was going to protect and rescue me. I didn't need my own light, I didn't need my own map. Why? Because I was stupid. Because I was arrogant, and because I had no idea what it was really like to be well and truly lost.

Back in Papua, the truth was I was spiritually lost and didn't know it. I was discovering as the years passed that there was a thirst inside me that no romance, nor adventure, nor challenge could quench. But I didn't understand this longing. I didn't know why I felt so empty and alone inside. I didn't know what was behind it, what the purpose was, what drove those feelings that haunted me. I didn't know how to climb out of the darkness I felt inside me. It was like trying to find my way out of that cave without a light.

Can you bind the beautiful Pleiades? Can you loose the cords of Orion?

Can you raise your voice to the clouds and cover yourself with water?

What is the way to the place where lightning is dispersed, or the place where the east winds are scattered over the earth?
—God

WHEN THE SHARKS COME

There comes a time in everyone's life when we feel the compelling of God Almighty to reach into the blackness of our hearts, find that small glimmer of light, and pull on it as hard as we can until it turns our soul inside out.

It was fairly common for us to go beach camping at one of our favorite beaches in West Papua. Uncle Wally and I went every weekend we could get free. We would load up the old diesel truck with the usual assortment of tarps and ropes, sleeping bags, fishing gear, Hawaiian slings, kerosene lanterns, food, snorkel gear, Uncle Wally's two kids Jared and Jacinda, and whoever else wanted to tag along. On this particular occasion, I was the only kid, and my dad was with us. We had a late start and drove the forty-five minutes of winding jungle road in the dark to the coastal town of Depapre. This is where we met Marawai who would take us the rest of the way on his boat.

It was getting late by the time we reached the beach. We unloaded all the gear and went about making a quick camp. Light the kerosene pressure lanterns, lay a tarp on the ground, string a tarp to cover it for a roof, bring all our supplies up from the beach, collect driftwood for a fire and we had a camp.

The plan was to gear up, get into the water, spear some fish and lobster, come back, shower in the jungle waterfall, cook some of our catch in the fire, have a snack and go to sleep. It was a great plan, pretty much the same plan we had every campout.

There were no moon or stars shining on the ocean that night. The darkness hung like a black drape from the heavens to the sea. We strapped a couple pressure lanterns (pressurized kerosene lanterns that you pump and that burn bright for a long time) to a six-foot dugout canoe with bamboo outriggers. Dark nights were the best for lobster hunting because the moon wouldn't cast a shadow from the hunters and alert our prey. The light from the pressure lanterns would be enough to see the red reflections of the lobster's eyes.

I was fairly new to night diving, having only done it a couple of times, and I was a little bit scared, to say the least. Spear fishermen have a lot of stories about sharks. Not all of them end well. If you want to die from a shark bite, go spear some fish and carry them on a string through the ocean in the middle of the night. It's not the shark's fault if you're stupid. To avoid that, we would put the fish in a canoe. We weren't that stupid...at least not until underwater flashlights came out.

I was incredibly curious about sharks and shark behavior. Since I shared the ocean with them, I wanted to understand these creatures. I had read every article and watched every documentary that I could find. The main things I knew were that sharks had poor eyesight, sharp teeth, an uncanny sense of smell and a hypersensitivity to vibrations, which guided them more than their vision. I always had a healthy respect for them even though it wasn't until years later that I began to really appreciate the very important role they played in the health of the ocean.

I thought of them now as we were entering their world at feeding time. *"The perfect killing machine,"* someone with a British accent was narrating in my head. *"The fool steps unwittingly into the shark infested waters...spear fishing is the most dangerous activity one can engage in whilst in tropical waters."* I shivered as the cold saltwater crept up my bare chest and over my ears.

Spear or no spear, sharks clearly held the advantage over me in the water, especially considering the absence of light. If you've ever seen a shark up close it is a fascinating experience. Second only to manta rays, in my opinion, they are phenomenally graceful to watch. With sharks I found that while fear sets in and tells you to get out of the water there is a strange magnetism, an almost hypnotic spell they cast, that makes it impossible to take your eyes off them. Many times I found myself following them if I spotted them in daylight hours.

Marawai stayed behind on the beach while we swam out through a small passage in the reef that encircled the lagoon. I suppose Marawai was first a fisherman rather than an underwater hunter. I can recall the night he stood on the bow of his boat. With a bamboo spear in hand and the boat on plane he picked off a couple squid in the dark water with surgical precision.

Breakers thundered over the reef walls around us as we allowed ourselves to be sucked out through the channel.

The sea seemed particularly angry with us that night and finding lobsters proved difficult. However, we managed to spear a number of fish as we headed out, farther and farther away from land. Our lantern cast an eerie glow around the canoe, a ten-foot diameter net of light that sank only twelve feet deep at best.

A black silhouette gracefully glided beneath me then disappeared into the darkness from which it came. The shark began to appear in and out of the shadows, again and again. Was it one shark or several sharks? I remembered Uncle Wally telling me about the time a ten-foot shark sideswiped him one night. I was glad it wasn't me! That's all I could think about now as I watched the gray creature and tried to guess his intentions.

I was entranced and momentarily distracted from gaining control over my growing apprehension. I knew very well that it wasn't so much the shark you could see that you had to worry about; it was the shark that you couldn't see. Victims of shark attacks rarely saw them coming. Surprise attack was the favorite weapon of the shark, to incapacitate and inflict the greatest amount of damage with the first bite.

Uncle Wally never seemed to be worried about the sharks. At least he wouldn't say if he was. "Sharks are everywhere!" he'd say with a wicked grin by the fire light, picking his teeth with a large dive knife. Marawai would raise his eyebrows and chuckle. I wondered if that was supposed to make me feel better. It felt like I was being raised by pirates, which was okay by me.

The waves were getting worse as we swam farther and farther away from shore. Whenever a fish was speared, we quickly tossed it into the canoe. Still, I could see them bleed-ing into the water and I knew the sharks lurking nearby could smell the blood. I felt extremely uncomfortable with the whole situation—I felt very much out of my element. The first movie that made a lasting impression on me as a child was *Black Stallion*. The scene when the boat sinks at night and the kid is left to fight for his life in the ocean was seared into my brain. I always thought that would be the worst thing that could ever happen to me.

It terrified me.

I was freaking myself out. If you're around sharks and it's dark and you're scared and then they disappear, you start hearing the theme song from *JAWS* in your head.

The fear in me was growing and I couldn't concentrate. The ocean started to annoy me. I was getting frustrated as it tossed me this way and that. To really enjoy the ocean, you have to feel like it's for you, not against you. When it feels like it's against you, you can't win. Everything looked gray, like an old movie. I had a bad feeling about this night. I wanted to go back, but it was too late. We'd moved too far beyond the opening in the passage for me to swim back alone safely. Besides, I wasn't about to leave the glow of the lanterns that were providing light from their perch on the canoe.

Suddenly, I felt myself being launched into the air, then drug under the water like a rag doll. I felt the weight of the water on me, pounding me into the coral. What was happen-ing? I held my breath. I did not want to die by drowning! I didn't want to end up like one of the victims of the *Lucky Catch*. I didn't want to wind up in a body bag. Or have someone else have to pack up my clothes and send them back to my mother. I saw flashbacks of my name on the *Lucky Catch* sign-up list, taped to the wall. Was this my time to go? It didn't look good for me.

Had the soul predator finally come for me, that mysterious angel of death? Or perhaps it was a just a really big shark? I didn't want to spend my last few minutes of consciousness looking at gnashing jaws and watching my limbs being ripped off. Instinctively I checked my arms and legs. No, I wasn't bit, I had been caught in a rogue wave. The water had been sucked off the reef and we had been caught on the crest of it. The wave pulled us up into its mighty hand and then smashed us down onto the reef, scattering us like broken ships on the rocks.

Everything was happening so fast. *Which way was up?* I looked at the bubbles… they weren't going up, they were swirling around and around my head… *C'mon! You can figure this out,* I told myself. The coral was at my back…or was it? I waited until the worst of the wave had passed, then pulled my feet under me and pushed off the reef. I could feel the familiar burning sting of coral cutting into my legs. I broke through the surface with a gasp, looking all around frantically to get my bearings. There was nothing but darkness. I lifted up my hand in front of my face and to my alarm I couldn't see it. I might as well have been blind.

Where was everybody? I shouted and shouted, but the only sound that returned to me was the thunderous pounding of the waves. I was alone…in the dark…out at sea.

I felt around with my feet to see if I could touch the reef. No, it was too deep. I reached out with my arms instinctively to grab something to hold me up out of the water. There was nothing. Wave after wave crashed over my head. I tried to turn away from them only to get another mouthful of saltwater. I choked and gagged and struggled to keep my head high enough out of the water. I pulled my mask off my face to try and get the water out of it and wiped my eyes. The salt stung. I started to lose it and thrashed around in frustration, I was wasting energy.

THINK! THINK! Don't panic! The worst thing you can do in the ocean is panic. I said it all the time. I had to get control of my fear. I tried to calm myself down. I focused on one task at a time. Clear the mask, put it back on. Clear the snorkel and put it back in my mouth and breathe. The mask blocked the waves and the snorkel allowed me to breath deeper without mouthfuls of water if I was careful. I took time to focus on my breathing and let the waves take me up and down as I floated on top. I wondered if my dad, Uncle Wally, and the two other guys had survived. Maybe they were injured? There was nothing I could do for anyone else. I had to think of what to do next.

There's nothing like bobbing about in the sea alone at night with sharks circling around to make your prayers sincere. My dear friend, Apa, the old fisherman from Rotuma likes to say in his gravelly voice, "Ohhh, when the sharks come, you really pray from the heart!" He was speaking from experience, having been shipwrecked so many times with hardened sailors. He would say, "Oh, you know those hard sailors, those who swear and curse God. They have the sweetest prayers when the sharks come. They pray like they've been in church their whole life. It's amazing!" I've since had thoughts of a two-step program to improve any-one's prayer life: the first step is to throw you in a small swimming pool, and the second is to add a tiger shark. There's got to be people who would pay for that.

I had studied other religions, but at the moment I was pretty sure neither Buddha, Mohammed, nor a million Hindu gods were going to save me. My thoughts turned to the God of the Bible. This God that supposedly had a plan for me. Maybe I would meet him soon. Maybe that shark would drag me through that door and I would find out for certain who was on the other side.

Suddenly I was brought back to my senses by some-thing slimy bumping my chest. I grabbed it. It was a dying parrot fish. *What the…?* There was another and another… I was surrounded by dead and dying fish that had spilled out of the canoe when the wave hit. I had to get out of this bloody mixture of dead fish and guts or I was going to be food for the sharks. I looked all around me, it was useless, I couldn't see anything.

Heading in a random direction, I tried to put some dis-tance between me and the blood spill. *Thunk!* I bumped into the canoe, it had indeed capsized. I felt around like a blind man, I knew from the joint of the wood that I was on the corner where the bamboo outrigger was attached to the sta-bilizing crosspiece that ran to the canoe. It was something to hold on to. For the first time since the lights went out, something good. Unless there were still dead fish trapped in the canoe. I pulled myself up on the outrigger trying to be one with the wood. I put all my weight on it to see if I could flip it but the suction was too great and I wasn't heavy enough. Perched on the upside-down outrigger, I finally had time to think of what I was going to do. Shouting for the others had proved futile so my thoughts turned to the bitter reality of surviving the night at the mercy of the sea. I reckoned there were about six hours of darkness left. I thought it might be smart to stay with the canoe. Perhaps in the morning I could find a way to turn it over. I prepared myself mentally to outlast the night and I prayed earnestly and from the heart like I had never prayed before.

"God, if you're real...save me."

> *God has made my heart faint; the Almighty has*
> *terrified me. Yet I am not silenced by the darkness,*
> *by the thick darkness that covers my face.*
> —Job

THE LIGHT

I don't know how long I drifted with the capsized canoe. I had my legs wrapped around one of the smooth bamboo outriggers of the canoe and was resting on the cross bar. Maybe I could convince the sharks that I was driftwood. As I drifted I halfway expected one to come by and take a nibble to find out. In any case, I wasn't expending any physical energy at the moment. Just going where the current was taking me, wherever that was, hopefully toward land and not out to sea, but I had no control over that.

I had given up calling for help some time ago. It felt useless because the roar of the pounding waves was so loud. But I must have drifted away from the reef and the noise enough to hear a faint sound in the distance. I gathered myself and pushed my head as high out of the water as I could.

It was Uncle Wally's voice in the distance. It was the first I had heard from any of my other companions. My dad was out there somewhere, along with Uncle Wally and two Papuan men. It sounded like he was shouting something about a light, but Uncle Wally's words were muffled in the crashing of the waves. I looked around me. I could not see the silhouette of land against the sky, I could not see a light and I could not see the direction of the waves. I could not see anything. Every trick I had learned about finding your way in the sea at night was useless.

Then suddenly and more clearly, there it was again. "Swim to the light! Swim to the light…" Uncle Wally's voice trailed off and then it was gone.

I had a flashback to the time Uncle Wally and I took some Americans out spearfishing one night. Instead of swimming out from a beach like we normally did, we had anchored on an unfamiliar reef far from land. We left a bright pressure lantern on the boat so that we could find it again and took the small canoe with us to put the fish in. These amateurs were so inexperienced that one of them ended up accidently spearing Uncle Wally in the leg when Uncle Wally tried to stop him from unwittingly capsizing our canoe. Uncle Wally pulled me aside to let me know that he had been skewered. He didn't want his guests to feel bad but he wasn't sure how bad he was bleeding.

"We should get you back to the boat," I said.

Uncle Wally whispered back in a hushed voice, "About that…" his voice breaking into a quiet laugh.

I let out a snort like he was about to tell me a funny joke.

"Do you have any idea where we left the boat?" He asked, chuckling.

"Hahaha! That's a good one!" It was really hard not to laugh out loud. "Why are we laughing? That's not really funny," I sputtered through my snorkel. Clearly the light we had left on the boat had gone out for some reason. *"Are you serious?"* Uncle Wally was known to pull a few practical jokes on people. "Uh…" I looked around, "I think it was that way," I pointed.

"Ok," he said, "let's go see if we can find it before these guys realize what's going on."

Fortunately that night there was enough light from the moon to see the white paint of the boat in the distance and we were able to find it, fix the lantern and get Uncle Wally's leg patched up. I was not sure my current plight would turn out so well. At the very least, I wasn't laughing. I wished Uncle Wally was with me now and we could think of something funny to say about *this* situation.

The thought of seeing a light now began to get my hopes up. What light? Straining my eyes, I thought I could make out a tiny orange light in the distance. I fought to keep my eyes on it and not lose sight of it in the rolling waves. *What if it's a ship?* I wondered. I could end up swimming out to sea! Distance is difficult to judge on the ocean, especially at night. I tried to think clearly.

Think, Ray, think.

Wait, I thought… if it were an electric light it would be yellow or white. This light was orange which must mean fire, and if it is fire it would have to be on… land!

I swam toward the light, and took the canoe with me, pushing it in front of me as I kicked with my fins. I believed I was away from the all the dead fish by now, but I wasn't sure. There was a lot of splashing around me, but I couldn't tell if it was waves against the reef or waves against the canoe hull, or sharks or what? I really couldn't see anything at all, but with that light to focus on, I was now on a mission to get there and I put all my other fears behind me.

It was critical for me not to lose sight of the orange glow; it was my only hope, my salvation. Every minute seemed like an hour when all I could think about was getting out of the predicament I was in. It was slow going but it wasn't as strenuous as I thought. I was wearing fins, and the boat seemed to be moving along well with me. Maybe the current was in my favor, maybe I had help from unseen hands.

But soon I heard the familiar rumbling of the waves on the reef that encircled the lagoon around our beach and campsite. I knew that sound very well. I had fallen asleep to the rhythm of those waves dozens of times. The sound of the waves coming into the lagoon was very distinctive. First you would hear a roar as the initial wave crashed over the coral walls, and then you could hear it roll in and up on the sand. Crash! Rumble! Sssssss, Crash! Rumble! Sssssss. If you listened closely enough you could hear the shells and broken coral rolling up the beach with the wave and then back down again. I was nearly there. My fear all but gone now, I knew if I didn't find the reef entrance I was going to get thrashed on the reef for a second time that night. I was suddenly aware of my bruised body. *Who cares*, I thought, *I've got to get to land.*

What I didn't know was that Marawai, wise old fisherman that he was, saw our lights go out and had lit a bonfire on the beach. He chose a location right in front of the passage entrance, so as we made our way to shore we could come in safely through the channel. By carefully following the light, I found myself right in the channel mouth. Water rushed out the channel from the lagoon and was dumped back in over the reef by the waves. I had to kick hard against the current using the surge of the waves for momentum to get in but once into the lagoon all was calm. The crash and the rumble were behind me, the soft "sssss" of the waves lapping the beach in front of me.

As I gave the canoe a few last pushes and approached the light of the fire I noticed Uncle Wally and another diver were already on the beach. I could see their silhouettes by the fire as they spoke to Marawai, no doubt filling him in on the details of our adventure. I could almost make out what Uncle Wally was saying just from his hand gestures. The experienced men by the fire watched us as we approached, noting that we all were accounted for.

My head was fuzzy from lack of sleep and exertion, but as I strained to see through the mind fog my dad and the fourth diver appeared in focus at the opposite far corners of the canoe outriggers; they had been with me for some time but I had no idea how long they'd been hanging on because of the darkness. Apparently we had all had the same experience calling out for the others and then giving up and finding the canoe, but each at an opposite corner of an outrigger.

Upon reaching shallow water and planting my feet in the sand, a feeling of comfort and relief washed over me as I realized we were all safe. A tropical breeze swept through the palm trees firmly rooted in solid ground above the beach and chilled me at the same time. Our tasks were now more menial. We tended to the canoe, flipping it over and dragging it out of the water to the high tide mark. The lanterns were ruined and our catch was gone, but other than that we were okay.

I didn't want the others to know how scared I had been

so I didn't make a big deal about it. Nobody seemed to want to talk, everyone was tired and thought only of warmth and sleep now. These were tough men, hardened by the sea and by life itself. I could appreciate the fact that they never showed weakness or fear or even over concern for me. It made me feel like a man, not a kid. It made me feel like everything was going to be fine.

I sat down and took my fins off, taking my time and listening to the waves crash on the reef. Then slowly I trudged my way up the beach and collapsed beside Marawai's fire. I lay there for a while, gazing up at the starless sky. I was completely drained, not so much physically but emotionally and psychologically. I had honestly convinced myself that I was going to die a horrible death that night.

Uncle Wally and some of the other guys were already putting away their dive gear, sweeping sand off the tarp we would be sleeping on, pulling out sleeping bags and getting ready for bed.

I reflected on everything that had just happened. I felt that God had saved us. I thought about him, God.

"What's the deal with you, God? What do you want from me?"

In my heart I felt him speak to me very clearly:

"This…what just happened to you…is your life. You are living in darkness, with no hope, no light and no direction. You are hopelessly lost and you cannot save yourself. You are helpless and you will die like this if you don't do something. The devil is like the shark, he is at home in this darkness. He will eventually find you, drawn to you by the stench of your disobedience, and he will destroy you. You won't even see him coming. But I have given you a way to reach the other side safely. I have left you a light to find your way home. That light is the light of Jesus Christ. Follow him and you will never walk in darkness."

These words pierced my heart. I was ready. It was time.

I answered him, "God, if Jesus is the light, I will follow him. I know what it's like now to be lost without hope, I understand the fear and the helplessness. I don't ever want to experience that again. I will follow him even when the waves are high and rough; I won't look to the right or the left. I will keep my eyes steady. From this day forward, you will be my God."

I knew from the Bible that we humans had sinned against God by rebelling against him and the kind of life he intended us to live, and that the penalty for our sins was going to be death. Not just a physical death, but a spiritual death as well. I knew one day there would be a reckoning and that God, because he is holy and just, would have to come back and judge us all accordingly. I knew that God had sent Jesus into the world as a beacon of hope because he would be the sacrifice for our sins. I knew that if we chose to put our faith in him, we would be given grace and forgiveness and the promise of eternal life. His sinless perfection would be passed on to us to cover our sinful imperfection so that we would be able to stand before God almighty with confidence that we were clean and pure, and therefore free from the eternal judgment and penalties that come with sin. What this meant was that death would no longer have power over me, as a pathway to damnation and destruction. Death would simply be a transition from this life into a heavenly eternity with God.

The reality of what I had experienced both physically and emotionally began to sink in, heightened by the spiritual analogy God had given me. I thought of all the poor souls lost to the sea. I thought of the fear and the helplessness they must have felt, the loneliness of their final hours and their prayers for salvation. Spiritually, it was no different.

I had tried to escape all these truths but I couldn't run from them anymore. God had been working on me, he had made himself known to me, he had made himself real to me, and he had rescued me.

I accepted it. I surrendered to it.

This was a monumental turning point in my heart and mind. It was the beginning of a journey, my *own* journey, my own walk with God. Not my parents', not the church's, not Uncle Wally's or anyone else's. Others had pointed me to the light, now it was my responsibility to follow it on my own.

There was a freshwater spring behind our camp on the beach and we had rigged up a shower out of hollowed out bamboo. I took a flashlight and a towel with me and made my way into the jungle to wash away all the salt from our dive. It was refreshing and invigorating and it made me feel alive. When I returned to the campsite, Marawai was roasting a fish over coals on the fire. He tore a piece of meat from its side and handed it to me without saying a word. I squatted beside the fire with him to warm up some more after my cold shower. The delicious warm food in my stomach was just what I needed. I took a sip of fresh water from a jug and lay down in my sleeping bag and slept like a baby.

~ ~ ~ ~ ~

Years later, when I was in college, I got the news that Marawai had passed away. When I returned to West Papua, Uncle Wally took me to visit his grave. It was a simple plot by the sea, underneath a mango tree. I remember looking around and thinking, "This is the kind of place I'd like to be buried." It was fitting for the old fisherman to be laid beside the water in such a beautiful place. I said my last goodbye to Marawai there under that mango tree. He had safeguarded my life on many an adventure.

He had always joked that I should stay and guard the beach, but he had really always been the capable, strong protector. "You're the guardian now," I whispered, just as he always had been.

The fire Marawai lit the night I ended up capsized and lost at sea not only led me to safety, it warmed my body just as hope warmed my heart. New life was breathed into my spirit. It was like I had been raised from the dead.

It was time for me to go from needing a light to being a light for others.

I am the light of the world.
Whoever follows me will never walk in darkness, but
will have the light of life.
—Jesus

RESCUE

Before I knew it, it came time for me to graduate from high school. In many ways I did not want to leave my home in Papua, things were finally rather good for me. My life was leveling out and I was pretty content. At the same time I knew it was a big world out there and I wanted to see it and experience new adventures. But I had no idea what I wanted to do with my life.

Uncle Wally suggested that I should decide what the most important thing in the world was for me and to pursue that. The simple answer to that question was that I wanted to be a light for others who had struggled to find their way through the darkness I had experienced. To do that I was going to have to build a strong foundation in my relationship with God. So I decided to participate in a discipleship program run by Youth with a Mission (YWAM). It didn't hurt that their program was located in Hawaii. I moved to Kona and spent the next year and a half in Hawaii with YWAM, which included practical service in China and Japan.

After completing a couple courses, I realized it was probably time to go see my family. By then my parents had relocated to Dallas, Texas. I wrestled with the decision to go to cowboy country, because I knew it was going to be a very "fish out of water" experience for me, quite different from the tropical life I knew and loved. I had no desire to trade my flip-flops for cowboy boots. I did not want to leave Hawaii at all, but I strongly felt it was something I needed to do. I ended up working in construction and taking classes at a community college in Dallas for a couple of years.

At this point in my life, I rekindled a long-ago ambition to work my way up to a Rescue Diver certification. I had never lost the desire to be a rescuer after watching the heroic divers doing their job in Canada for the families of the *Lucky Catch* victims. Although as far as water rescue goes, the dim reality is that it is more often a recovery operation by the time emergency services are called. Water rescues are few and far between, body retrieval more the norm. But I believed it was an important job after what I had witnessed at the tragic father/son outing. Families needed that closure; they needed to be able to bury their loved one in order to move on. I remember how agonizing it was for the families of the *Lucky Catch* to have to wait for word of a family member. As the days dragged on, they couldn't let go of hope even though there really was none left. There was always that chance that by some miracle their loved one had made it to shore and was merely lost. It was up to the divers to bring in that final confirmation.

I completed my rescue diver certification with PADI and then volunteered to be a rescue diver for the sheriff's department. They already had a full dive team so they put me on the search and rescue team instead. Undaunted, I continued to dive and waited for an opening on the team.

I'm not sure there was anything that scared me more than the water, or worse, looking for a dead body in one foot of visibility, but I wanted to be in control, and not be the victim gasping for air or for useless hope. I wanted to have a grip on the crisis, to be above it and not be broken by it. I wanted to confront it straight on and have the skill not only to conquer my fears but to master the environment. I wanted to be the rescuer, not the victim.

I would work hard during the year in Texas to save up enough money to return to Papua in the summers. There I could spend long summer days diving in the crystal clear Pacific ocean instead of the murky Texas lakes. The more I learned about diving and the ocean, the more I enjoyed it. My confidence grew the more I was educated. I've never lost my healthy respect for the sea; I know when to go and when not to go. I quite enjoy sharks now. I seek them out, I love to watch them, but you have to understand their behavior, you have to know when to get out. The same goes for the ocean, you have to know when it's not safe and respect that.

Then one day my grandfather called and offered to help me out with my tuition if I attended a small school in northwest Arkansas. Perhaps he saw sending me to an accredited college as an investment in his legacy. I had definitely shown interest in overseas missions by this time. But Arkansas? In the middle of the continental United States? As beautiful as Arkansas was, I was not excited about moving farther inland to a landlocked state. I couldn't understand why my path was leading me so far away from the ocean that I loved.

It wasn't long after I settled into life in the Ozarks that I realized I was there for a reason. A beautiful reason, and she sat behind me in biology class. A girl caught my attention with her sparkling blue eyes, genuine smile, wisdom, character and love for God. We became friends, which led her to pursue an opportunity to spend a summer in Papua for a school internship. That seemed like a pretty good opportunity for me to go back with her and show her my little world.

Each of us got internships in Papua for our degrees in Intercultural Studies and Community Development—my major and Laura's minor. My job was to assist my local counterpart in a series of workshops introducing education in sanitation and clean water for one of the Papuan villages. The goal was to reduce 80% of disease in the village by implementing more sanitary conditions and behavior. Laura's assignment sent her to another village to work with a missionary nurse.

During the week I would call Laura on the jungle radio. Apparently all the other missionaries would listen in on the radio hour for entertainment. Each station had a chance to check in with main base in town with any business they needed to attend to whether to talk with someone or make arrangements for planes, doctors and what not, but the conversations were broadcasted on the airways for all to hear. I suppose conversations between the two young lovebirds was the only kind of soap opera they were going to get in the jungle.

Before we headed out to our respective outposts Laura and I had several weeks together where I got to show her around my stomping grounds. We returned to the infamous beach where I had my shark encounters and I shared my great memories of that place with her: the fishing trips with Marawai and how much I missed him. Other interns joined us as we all camped on that same beach where God had rescued me.

Laura got to see and experience what I loved about this tropical home of mine, and the sea. I was at home here, at ease and comfortable. She could see the difference from the awkward person I was in the USA, trying to fit into American college life. That wasn't really me… this was me. The mysterious beauty of Papua, like a drug that ran through my own veins, worked its magic on her and we fell deeply in love under the palm trees and stars. Laura had seen the ocean in my eyes and loved me for it and in it.

POINT OF NO RETURN

The shiny blue and white helio courier crawled across the sky, dodging clouds above the magnificent green jungle below. I could see flocks of white cockatoos soaring over the trees and the occasional hornbill with its mighty black wings that sounded like a pterodactyl if you've ever had one fly over you. The little plane dropped its flaps and descended into the thick layer of humidity that hung over the tree canopy of West Papua like dragon breath. Towering trees licked our wheels until a dirt runway appeared out of nowhere. The plane dropped purposefully into the opening in the forest and rumbled up the short runway to a halt by a small radio shed made from split logs with a crooked antennae sprouting out of the top of it. The local tribal people gathered around the plane excited to see what the big blue bird had brought this time.

As Jack, my local counterpart, and I stepped out of the tiny doorway of the plane into the crowd I surveyed the humble surroundings of the village and the missionary outpost. There were a hodge podge of huts scattered on the side of the runway among banana trees. The familiar smell of cooking fires hung low in the trees. There was something always beautiful and comforting to me about seeing the smoke over the villages, a few scraggly dogs used for pig hunting and the odd uncatchable chicken under a bamboo hut. The people had very few worldly possessions, little clothing, and a few personal items that they carried with them. There were the typical net bags woven from jungle vines that the women hung from their foreheads on their backs, often with a baby inside, warm and cozy like a tree kangaroo in a pouch. And the men bare chested with their bow and arrows on their shoulders either on their way to hunt or returning. They came up to me with a warm welcome and rubbed my white arms, especially fascinated with my furry blond arm hair. I would be stationed here for the next few weeks as a part of my college internship.

In the following days as we surveyed the situation and spoke to the villagers, we could see the concern the missionaries had for better sanitation. There was an unusual amount of skin disease as well as a variety of other health issues. I had always wanted to help people with their basic needs, in practical ways with what resources were available to me. There wasn't always funding and resources to help, but there was still a lot that could be done with my access to information. In this case, it was just beginning with the knowledge of what a basic germ was and how to protect themselves better from diseases. Such a simple concept with such huge ramifications.

It didn't take us long to learn that their understanding of sickness and disease was more closely related to the spirit world than to biology and the physical realm. In order to teach them a whole new way of thinking we had to address the old way as well. One of the biggest challenges we had with introducing outhouses was that the people believed evil spirits inhabited the small rooms with bad smells. I didn't have a problem believing that. I had one in my bathroom growing up. In order to get around this we went with a design that incorporated their idea of bigger spaces so they wouldn't feel claustrophobic and eliminated the bad smell by piping waste to a septic type system. In the end, working together, listening to one another and having a willingness to understand each other's point of view, led to a mutually beneficial solution that the villagers were happy with and worked well for them.

The people in this quaint little village beside a beautiful river were very generous to us, sharing what little food they had: bats, tree kangaroos, and all sorts of strange birds they had hunted from the forest. One day one of the villagers brought me some "bat soup." It was literally a bowl of soup with a small bat floating in it. Like he had accidently fallen into the bowl and drowned. I poked the black furry body with my finger and it bobbed up and down. I looked at the grinning man, and wondered to myself if they actually ate that or if this was a joke they were playing on me. They took me hunting with them, showed me places they loved and taught me about their way of life. When I went with the local people into the jungle, I never took anything with me or worried about fire, water, food or shelter. I had 100% confidence that they could survive with what was around them and take care of me as well. In this way they were incredibly rich.

However, one particular night around 2:00 a.m. we were awakened by a mob at our door. I peeked through the window at the commotion outside and saw a crowd of people gathered with fire torches. Jack had become like a brother to me in our months in the jungle. He had some experience with this tribe and spoke the trade language fluently.

"What's going on, Jack?" I whispered in the dark.

Jack went to the door, then came back to get me.

"They want us to come with them," he said. "Something's wrong."

I could tell by the demeanor of the people gathered outside that whatever was happening, it wasn't good. By now the whole house was awake. The missionaries' daughter came with us as she seemed to understand the situation better than we did.

"A baby is sick," she said, as we hiked behind the orange glow of torches through the forest. I had no idea what to expect. We followed the winding trail of fire until we came to a simple hut outside the village and were ushered inside with great urgency. The floor and walls were made of bamboo. There was nothing to speak of in the hut other than a small shell containing some oil that made a candle-like glow illuminating a very young mother in the center of the room holding a small baby boy in her lap. He was struggling to breathe.

I sat beside the mother while Jack and the missionaries' daughter spoke to her and the others, trying to make sense of what was going on. People still stood around outside while some had come in, their faces glowing in the dim light of the oil lamp, all looking at us and at the baby. I listened to the conversation and tried my best to figure out what was being said.

Eventually Jack leaned over and explained. "The baby is very sick. They say he will die tonight if we don't pray to our God to save him. They want us to pray. They brought us here to pray."

"What's wrong with the baby?" I asked.

"Can't breathe," he said. "They say he will die."

"Let me have a look," I said. I examined the baby and indeed he was struggling to breathe. I checked the airway, it was clear. *How do they know the baby will die tonight?* I asked myself.

"Look, Jack. Why does he have to die? We can save this baby. We can keep him alive till dawn and then we'll call a plane and get him to a hospital. This is just some kind of virus, just a cold, maybe whooping cough or something like that. It's got to be totally treatable. All we have to do is keep him breathing for a couple more hours till the sun comes up, then we can get help."

Jack said, "This is a big deal. He is her only child. Her husband has left her; this is a male child and one day he must take care of her. He's her whole future in this village. She needs him to live. That's why they called us to pray... She is desperate."

I turned to look at the mother and child as Jack shared how important it was for this child to live. I'm not one to sit on my hands.

"Get me a sheet from the house and boil some water," I directed. The request was translated and a runner went for the sheet, a pot of water was put on to boil. Soon the sheet was handed to me and we had a basin of boiled water. People were looking at me puzzled as I gathered the odd items together.

"Jack, tell them we're going to put the mother and child under this sheet with the steam from the water and hope it helps him to breathe better."

We all sprung into action and got the mother and baby under the sheet. We monitored the breathing and to our great joy it seemed to be working! He was taking deeper breaths. An hour had gone by and the child was still alive.

C'mon kid, fight!

Daylight and salvation were within reach now. We were prepared to radio for an emergency flight as soon as the radio operator came on at first light. Time was going by so slowly now. We were on the edge of our seats.

After some time we noticed the baby's breathing was getting more difficult again. They took the sheet off and said, "We really want you to pray. Pray to your God that you've been telling us about. The one who is greater than the evil spirits that cause sickness and death. Pray that he will let this child live."

Jack looked at me, and asked seriously, "Will you pray the child will live?"

"You pray, Jack! You're Charismatic! When you pray the earth shakes!"

It was true, I'd been praying with Jack every day. The man could pray. If anyone could get God's attention it was going to be Jack, I was sure of that.

So he did. He prayed a mighty prayer. It was powerful, out there in that little hut amidst the ancient trees in the dark hours of the early morning, in defiance of all evil spirits of the jungle, in defiance of poverty, and sickness, and ill fortune of being born into such a remote place with no access to the basic necessities to ensure your precious child would live. It was unfair and God was just, so he had to respond, he had to. Jack finished his prayer. There was no change in the breathing of the baby.

"Your turn," Jack said softly as he handed me the baby.

I gazed at that little baby in my hands. A tear from my eyes fell on his chubby little cheek. The reality of these people's sufferings was starting to become very real to me. How hopeless they must feel, when there's nothing you can do. When there is no access to things like medicine.

"Pray!" one of the men said in his native language.

"Ok, ok, I'm gonna pray... God... you see these people, you love these people. You love this child. Heal him, I pray. Let him live. Let him grow up and take care of his mother. We are all looking for you to come through on this one. We've been telling these people about you. Let them see you are real and that you hear them..."

As I said, "Amen," I could feel the life leaving the baby's body. It was surreal. I could feel his soul leave that body light and empty in my hands. I wanted to reach up and grab it and bring it back. No, this was unacceptable! I felt all hope leave with that soul. There was a moment of complete and utter silence as we all realized what just happened.

Before I could come to my senses, the mother snatched the child from my arms and exploded into blood curdling wails of grief. Cries went up from the whole group, ripping through the jungle, screams in the darkness. The mother dropped the body on the floor, grabbed a knife and tried to stab it into her heart. The hut exploded with chaos. Several people leapt on her and fought with her to pry the knife from her hands. Men sprang into the small hut with vines to tie up the grieving mother.

I was beside myself in grief and horror. I didn't know what was happening. The lifeless body of the child was being stepped on in the chaos. Jack and the missionaries' daughter grabbed my arm and pulled me outside the hut.

"What the... what!?" I bent over, trying to catch my breath and clear my head. "What is happening?"

"She will try to kill herself until the sun comes up so she can help the child find his way to the afterlife," the girl explained. "The others will try to stop her, tie her up with vines if they have to. She will not stop until dawn. Once the sun comes up, if she's still alive, she will accept it."

We walked back to the mission house but we could not sleep as we listened to the wailing for the rest of the night.

I could not understand why God did not answer our prayers. I was angry at him, really angry. "What am I doing out here?" I yelled at God. "I tried to do something meaningful with my life. I gave up the comforts of America to come here, I gave up my job and the ability to make money, I sold my car to buy a plane ticket. I have nothing to go back to, I gave it all to come and help these people, to make a difference in the world."

"I'm not making a difference," I cried, "I'm just adding to the misery!"

I had seen too much. Where was God? If God wasn't here, if he wasn't going to back me up, I didn't want to do this anymore. I wanted to go home. I was ready to turn my back on all of it, to put it in my rearview mirror and just get on living my own life the way I wanted without a conscience about what was happening to rest of the world. I wanted to go back to being ignorant about it all. That was my new plan.

When the sun came up, the wailing stopped and I must have drifted off to sleep. I heard a light knock at my door. Jack poked his head in, "They want to know if you want to go to the baby's burial."

"What?" It took me a minute to get my bearings. I had hoped the last night had just been a nightmare. But no, it was real. "Yeah, okay, I'm coming."

A villager came to get me and led me into the jungle to a clearing. The light shown through in magnificent golden streaks that lit up a green meadow where butterflies danced on purple flowers. I saw the mother standing humbly with another woman, the missionary and two men with a shovel. A small wooden box lay on the ground with the baby inside. My heart broke all over again. I didn't know what to expect in this culture for a burial so I stood there quietly observing.

There seemed to be an argument with the men with the shovel. I asked what was going on. The missionary explained that the woman had to pay them to dig a hole and they couldn't agree on a price. Indignant, I approached the man with the shovel.

"Give it to me!" I was being rude but I didn't care. I was tired and I was broken. We were burying a baby in the forest and I didn't understand why the mother should have to pay to dig a hole, and I didn't care. I would do it.

I took the shovel from him and began to dig. With every scoop, tears fell on that little grave. This wasn't a proper graveyard; there were no markers or tombstones here. It didn't seem right.

The older woman leaned over and said matter of factly, "I have five babies buried here."

That did it, I couldn't hold back anymore. I cried with each shovel full of dirt. I finished digging the hole and bent down to pick up the little canoe shaped box. The tribe believed the canoe would take their departed souls down the river to the afterlife. I gently placed the little box into the hole. *There shouldn't have to be boxes this small.* I thought back to only a few hours earlier when that beautiful boy was warm in my hands. My face was wet with dirt and tears. I didn't know how much more of this I could bear.

At that moment a man came running out of the jungle into the little clearing. He spoke quickly to the missionary. The man was an uncle to the mother and had run all the way from the next village as soon as he heard the news. The baby's great uncle also happened to be a new Christian.

The missionary asked the uncle to say a prayer before I covered up the little box with mud. The man humbly accepted and prayed a most beautiful prayer:

"Father, we thank you that you loved this baby boy so much that you chose to free him from a life of suffering here to be by your side, to grow up in the house of a king."

That was exactly what I needed to hear. The perspective of hope this new believer had. His perspective of eternity. He was able to see beyond the suffering and beyond the circumstances, and even death, that God was indeed still in control and good through it all. I envied him; I should be reflecting the same peace and hope that he had. He was right and my attitude was completely off. Who was I to question God? Regardless, I struggled for a long time to accept what happened. It took me many years to get over it, in fact.

When he finished his prayer I covered up the little box with soil and we melted back into the jungle, leaving the meadow to the golden rays of sunshine and butterflies.

When it came time for Jack and me to leave the village, the mother who lost her baby that night came to the airstrip to say goodbye. Through a translator she told me as she squeezed my hands tight, "Now that you've seen us, you can never forget us. Now that you've seen our suffering you have to come back and help us."

Her words haunted me like that fateful night. It was true. I was never the same. I couldn't go back to my day job in America and forget what I had seen. There were great needs in the world. I knew that I had to help, even if it was just in some small way. I had to continue to give, I had to continue to go, I had to continue to pray, I had to do whatever was in my power to help alleviate suffering. That little baby's life was going to matter. Because of him, I was a different person. He put me on a path of no return.

RIDING THE WAVE

Straddling the surfboard, I looked down at my feet in the clear water off the coast of Kailua-Kona. The sun warmed my back as I enjoyed a conversation with my buddy Matt who was teaching me how to surf. To my right sat a girl in a silver bikini on a short board, to my left an old hippie on a long board. Both were friendly and pleasant to share the waves with. Surfing was much harder than I had anticipated, my arms were tired of paddling but I was contented. A few minutes earlier spinner dolphins had passed by several hundred yards away, jumping and playing. Life was good.

Looking back over the years behind me, there wasn't much else I desired right now. I was doing what I loved to do, floating in the tropical sea without a care in the world.

As I drifted with the current, I let my mind take me back to college in America and the day I asked Laura to marry me. I had planned an elaborate trip to Cancun because it was imperative to me that I propose to her in the ocean, in the crystal clear waters of some exotic tropical escape, and Cancun was the closest one that I could sort of afford.

I pressured Laura to get dive certified so we could dive

in Cancun. She had no idea what I was up to. I had secretly built a treasure chest out of old weathered fence pickets, wood burned some designs onto it so it would look like a pirate's chest and filled it with costume jewelry and shells. In the center I placed an oyster shell from Papua with a diamond ring inside.

Unfortunately the trip didn't work out at the last minute, but things were already in motion and I didn't want to prolong the proposal any more. I was ready to be married, the sooner the better. I was left no choice but to find a dive site somewhere nearby. The best I could come up with on short notice was a dive site I knew well—Possum Kingdom near Forth Worth, Texas. Yes, Possum Kingdom, the most exotic place in Texas. A host of interesting things had been sunken in the lake at Possum Kingdom for divers to explore, like a fire truck, some boats, sculptures. You never knew what you'd discover down there. Why not a pirate's chest?

My brother and his girlfriend were with us and we all geared up to dive. At the last minute, to distract Laura, I told her I forgot my fins and we had to go back to camp and get them. While we were away, my brother Jeff strategically placed my handmade treasure chest in its designated spot at thirty-five feet below the surface.

When Laura and I reached the shore, Jeff was already underwater. I told Laura we should go catch up with him, just swim to the dive buoy and follow it down. I had her follow the line that was tied to the treasure chest on the bottom. As we descended into the poor excuse for ocean waters, Laura looked confused when she saw the old treasure chest, and looked back at me with furrowed eyebrows. I laughed into my regulator, motioned to the treasure chest, and opened my eyes wide while making the hand signals to "OPEN IT!"

She looked back at the box and with hands shaking she slowly opened the old lid. Inside, the diamond caught the light of the sun above us and sparkled wildly. Fish started to nip at the ring, I thought I better hurry this along before one of them eats it. I picked the diamond out of the shell and placed it on her finger. She stared at it in shock. I pulled out my dive slate and wrote, "Will you marry me?"

"YES!" she wrote. She laughed into her regulator and took it out to kiss me.

We surfaced and I asked her, "Will you be my mermaid forever?" She said yes again. We kissed and the rest, as they say, is history. We were married and moved back to Hawaii shortly after. I always joke that God had to send me to Arkansas to find my wife because she was too stubborn to come to Hawaii on her own.

I hadn't wanted to leave Hawaii after my YWAM experiences, and I had prayed about it all those years before that God would confirm to me whether or not I should really make this move. In one of these times of prayer I had randomly opened my Bible to Genesis 28:15 and highlighted it. I honestly believed Hawaii was the perfect fit for me and I had no idea why God would lead me on to Texas and Arkansas, in the heartland of America and away from the ocean. But I trusted him.

Upon returning to Hawaii with my wife and an education and all the tools I needed to be equipped to serve God overseas, I opened my Bible again to that same spot I had highlighted seven years before. I reread the verse I had read back then when he told me to go. It reads, "I am with you and will watch over you wherever you go, and I will bring you back to this land. I will not leave you until I have done what I have promised you." I was blown away, and I was so grateful. God, knowing me and what I needed, so much better than I knew myself had perfectly prepared me for what lay ahead.

In my wife, I had finally found a life-long love to share these incredible experiences with, to walk the beaches, watch the sunsets, collect shells, serve others and discuss things eternal. We are very different but complement each other so well. She loves me and I love her and it is good. I remain so eternally thankful to have her in my life.

"Ray, this is your wave, bro!" Matt said enthusiastically.

I snapped out of my daydream and glanced over my shoulder to time the wave. I started paddling and felt the water pulling me slowly up the crest. When I reached the peak I leaned forward and hopped to my feet; the board slid effortlessly down the wall of the wave. *Wow! What a rush!* All the paddling was worth it; I loved the feeling of being one with the power of the waves.

When the wave played out I fell back into the warm water and let it wash over me, the leash snapped taut on my ankle and I swam up to the board. As I paddled back to the breakers my buddy cheered, the girl smiled enthusiastically, and the hippie clapped. They were genuinely happy for me, they knew the feeling very well.

Could life get any better?

A TIME TO DIE

We strapped the boards to the roof of the Jeep Cherokee and headed for home. My buddy and I sat shirtless in the car and slowly followed the ocean down Ali'i Drive back home. As we rounded a bend I noticed the dive shop on the corner and thought out loud, "I'd really love to get my Dive Master certification."

I had already been Rescue Diver certified for a number of years and Dive Master was the next step toward my Dive Instructor License. Hawaii seemed like a great place to do it.

The next weekend I enrolled in the Dive Master class. A mandatory physical was required before I could be accepted so I dropped into the clinic. The blonde nurse held my hand in hers and looked up at the ceiling, counting to herself. She looked at me puzzled and then started counting again. I shifted in my chair uneasily. "Has anyone ever told you that you have an irregular heart beat?" she asked.

"No."

"Are you sure?"

"Yes, I'm sure. I think I would have remembered that."

"I'm going to call in a doctor," she said. "Wait here."

What on earth was going on? I put my fingers where hers had been on my wrist, seemed all right to me. In a minute a doctor appeared and hooked me up to an EKG machine.

"Hm," he grunted as he looked over the results. When I looked up from the bed, there were two doctors looking over his shoulder, shaking their heads.

"What is it?" I stammered. "Something bad?"

The first doctor paused, then said, "Tomorrow you fly to Honolulu first thing in the morning to see a cardiologist."

When I saw the cardiologist in Honolulu he informed me he wanted to put me on a treadmill for a stress test. I didn't know what this was all about other than something irregular with my heartbeat.

"Don't worry," he said, "a lot of people have irregular heartbeats; we just need to rule some things out."

The next day the technicians hooked me up to a bunch of multi-colored wires and instructed me to start jogging on the treadmill. Several minutes later, they assured me everything was looking good.

"One more minute and you'll be done. Doing well."

Thirty seconds later a loud steady beeeeeeeep sounded and I watched my heart flat line on the monitor in front of me.

Beeeeeep, the siren resounded through my brain loudly. I could feel myself falling; my vision began to narrow as if I were looking into a tunnel. I heard yelling and clipboards hitting the floor, then everything was quiet except for the beeping.

So this was what death felt like.

It was quiet, I couldn't feel anything, the world started

to fade into black.

"…hello…hello…"

If only I could feel my feet in the warm ocean again, the rising and falling of the mighty sea beneath me… I hadn't said goodbye to Laura… Oh dear… I wish I could have met my children… they would have been beautiful I'm sure… Why hadn't I done more with my life? I could have done a lot more. God, I could have done so much more.

The soul shark was coming for me; I could hear him swishing through the darkness toward me. I was going to the other side now. I wasn't afraid, I was sad. Something didn't seem right… what about the poor? What about the people who were suffering and needed help… What about the lost? Who would go?

Who would go?

The shark was beside me now, the angel of death waited beside me.

God, can you hear me? Can you hear me?

"Can you hear me? Can you hear me?" Light slowly came back to my eyes, things were fuzzy. Who the heck was beating my chest?

"Ow."

"Can you hear me?" A doctor was hitting my chest. "Is the defibrillator ready?" he yelled at the technician.

"Right here!" The technician handed him the paddles.

I could feel the cold tile floor beneath my back, suddenly my vision became clear. The doctor was coming toward my chest with two electrically charged paddles vibrating with an eerie sound.

"Whoa! Hang on buddy!" I grabbed his wrists. "Where

you goin' with those?"

The doctor smiled and let out a loud sigh, "He's back! He's okay."

I looked up to see half a dozen people in white coats standing over me. The doctor helped me sit up and the others left the room shaking their heads. The technician looked a little shook up.

"Are you okay?" I asked.

"Are *you* okay?!" he blurted out.

"Yeah, what happened?"

The doctor helped me up from the floor and onto the exam table. He put the cold stethoscope on my chest, "Your heart stopped beating. You have Ventricular Tachycardia; you need an immediate heart operation. You could die any minute. If you collapse again, try to fall on something and maybe it will jump start your heart."

Yeah, right. I'll try to keep that in mind.

Before I knew it I was strapped naked to an operating table. The doctor cut into the artery in my groin and ran the instruments up the artery to the heart where he tried to cauterize the bad signal in my heart with a laser.

After four hours of unsedated surgery (I liken it to a torture chamber, strapped to the table, naked and spread eagle—no meds, no sedatives), the doctor threw down his equipment and stomped out of the room.

"That's a shame…" the nurse said, as if I wasn't there, "…he's so young."

"Hey! What the heck does that mean?" I yelled from the table.

The nurses finished cleaning up without a word and left

me alone to wait to be wheeled out on the gurney. In the next few hours I found out my case was "unfixable" and I would have to be on beta-blockers, a medication that would slow the beat of my heart so that it wouldn't stop, for the rest of my life.

Back home in Kona, the medication had such a negative effect on me; I could hardly move from the couch. I felt like I was barely alive. I could hardly walk, I couldn't work, I couldn't live any semblance of the normal life I once had.

One day I decided it was time to get out of the house. Laura and I went down to watch people complete the Ironman triathlon. The Kona Ironman is a 2.4-mile swim, a 112-mile bike ride, and a 26.2-mile run. As I leaned on Laura's arm and braced myself against the stone wall, I watched a man in his 80s cross the finish line. Not far behind him, a handicapped man raced his wheelchair across the line.

"Look at me," I hung my head, "I'm twenty-seven years old and I'm barely alive. I can't do this anymore. I'm quitting the medication and taking my chances."

"Call the doctor," Laura advised.

The next day I phoned the cardiologist in Honolulu. "Doc, I can't do this. I'm going off the medication."

"You'll die."

"I don't care, I'm not living anyway. Look, is there any way at all this problem can be fixed?"

The doctor let out a sigh, "Well, we don't have the most up-to-date equipment here, perhaps on the mainland…"

"Wait, are you saying with better equipment I could be cured?"

"Well it's possible, but I won't recommend it to the

insurance company to cover the cost."

"Why not?" I was confused. If there were a way to heal me then why wouldn't the doctor recommend it?

"I won't recommend it, absolutely not… I mean, how does that make me look?" With that he hung up the phone.

I was angry; I didn't care how it made him look, I wanted my life back. I prayed, "Lord, give me my heart back. Make this possible somehow."

I flew back to Honolulu and went to see the hospital administrator. I told her my story. She called the doctor, who still refused to sign off for a new operation on my heart. The administrator told me that she would look into it some more and get back to me.

That night Laura and I prayed fervently that the Lord would hear our prayers for my heart. Early the next morning I got a call saying the insurance company would cover the full cost of another surgery on the mainland. This time the doctors successfully ablated the faulty electrical signal in my heart and suddenly I had my life back again.

Lying in the recovery room, I felt like God was asking me, "Is your heart really mine?"

I had to think about it.

It was easy enough to say that it was, but I still struggled with doing life my way. I was young, tan, strong, in the prime of my life, living in Hawaii with my whole life in front of me. Things were good for me but the battle for my heart was not over. The battle between the forces of good and evil had not gone away. In the blink of an eye my heart could stop and there was nothing I could do about it. I had no control over whether I lived or died… it was up to God.

My life was literally in his hands.

I realized all the troubles I had been through, all the tragedies, all the countries I had been to, my personality and all my experiences were to prepare me for the plan God had for my life. Was I going to follow him in that plan or not?

There was a part of me that didn't want to go back to poverty-stricken countries, back to the kind of place I was feeling God was calling me to serve. I was pretty comfortable where I was. What about money? What about family? What about safety? What about planning for retirement? Every excuse I could think of came to mind. It was an ongoing battle within me.

In fact, I didn't know if I was even qualified for what he was asking me to do. I didn't think that he could or would want to use someone like me. I was too young, too undereducated, too poor myself, how was this all going to happen?

"Is your heart really mine?" came the words again.

"Lord, you have always been faithful to me."

"Then trust me."

My heart at peace, I totally surrendered. "I will do whatever you want me to do. I will go wherever you want me to go."

*I assure you and most solemnly say to you, unless a
grain of wheat falls into the earth and dies, it remains
alone (just one grain, never more). But if it dies, it
produces much grain and yields a harvest.*

—Jesus

THE BEGINNING

"Who's feeling lucky today?"

The red speedboat came to a stop beside the *Buckaroo* that floated lifelessly in the bay. Gretchen watched curiously as the "pirates" glared at us, poised to attack. I stood and squared up with the captain. Suddenly he held up a hand and signaled for his boys to stop.

"Who are you?" he yelled.

My life flashed before me and when it had passed before my eyes, I smiled. I wasn't afraid of this man, and I wasn't afraid of *Dakuwaqa*, the legendary shark demon of the deep who lived in his cave in the Somosomo Strait. While many islanders, especially in the old days, had placed their hopes in *Dakuwaqa* to light the way through the dangerous reef passages with his phosphorescent wake at night, I had my own source of light. I had a hope that was steadfast and eternal, one that wasn't unpredictable or a threat to me. The devil had tried to destroy me many times, but I had found a secret in my walk with God, to die to myself. I was already dead, dead to this world, dead to my sins, and alive in Christ, my soul was eternal now. My salvation was secure. My spirit would live eternally in a better world. They could kill the body, my earth suit, but they could not have my soul.

The chapters of my life to this point weren't chapters at all, they were a prelude to the real story, a story that could only begin with a death, my own. I'd learned the secret: I had to die to live. Not a physical death, but a spiritual death to the wrong things I held onto and my selfish desires. Once I accepted this truth and the gift of Jesus, believing in him and accepting his grace and what he did on the cross for me, I received the gift of life, for now and for eternity.

I had received it and I was ready to live it, not just here on earth where the world continued to rage against me, but in its original perfection in heaven with my Savior and my God. Would today be the day I finally met him?

The angel was near, biding his time in the crystal blue water below me. I had seen the light behind the door and I knew who and what awaited me. I didn't fear the soul predator any more; I was ready. Were I to disappear into the deep as so many of my friends had, the angel would take me in his hands and swim me to the other side, safe into the arms of God.

Who are you? The question took me back many years to the jungles of Papua when a soldier put a gun barrel up my nose and asked me the same question. It's hard to forget things like that, but this time I knew who I was. I wasn't just an adventurer, I wasn't just an athlete, I wasn't just an American on the outside, Asian on the inside; I was a child of God, adopted into his family, his servant, his hands and his feet to the world. This knowledge gave me a great peace and greater freedom.

In spite of this, I was also responsible for Gretchen and I would protect her as far as it was possible by me, even if I had to lay my life down for her. The captain's raised hand was all that stood between me and a potentially violent confrontation. You could cut the tension with a knife.

"Are you Ray?" he asked.

I thought for a second, *was it good to be Ray or bad to be Ray?* I wasn't sure in this case.

"Yes," I replied, my grip tightening on the club at my side.

"You're Ray, from Nasau Bay," he stated, as if I didn't know.

"That's right."

"I know who you are…" His demeanor softened. "Boys, boys, stand down. Mr. Ray, you have a nice day." He produced a broad smile. Taking the cue from their captain, and realizing that I wasn't a threat to their resources, the villagers relaxed, sat down again, smiled and waved. They pulled away from my boat and headed toward the beach where I had left my students.

"Hey, hey wait! Those people are with me," I shouted across to the boat.

"Okay, okay!" They captain smiled and gave me a thumbs up. They turned the boat and headed back out to the strait and around the point.

I pulled the start cord and the old Mercury fired right up. As we motored away, I knew it was not so much my name that had saved me, as it was who I was connected to. Had they attacked me, it would have been an attack on the Fijian community and families who had adopted me as their own. Had I simply been an individual, I would have been in danger, but my relationship with the surrounding islanders and communities had made me untouchable. Such was my relationship with God, as his son I was a part of a much bigger picture: a purpose, a family and a tribe of eternal significance. As long as I was a part of his family, he wasn't going to allow anything to happen to me he didn't want to. After all…he had plans for me.

The *Buckaroo* kicked up on plane, the ocean was so blue and beautiful. In front of me loomed the emerald green island of Taveuni; in my wake, all the lessons from my past. The sun shone warm upon my skin, the clouds swirled carelessly above me, thirteen students were on the beach being trained to work with the poor, and I had been willing to die for someone out of love. A smile came to my eyes from somewhere deep within. This was what it meant to be alive.

If you confess with your mouth that Jesus is Lord and
believe in your heart that God raised him from the dead,
you will be saved.
—Apostle Paul

RETURN TO EDEN

The power was off and it was hot. I tossed and turned in my bed with a fever of 104. The nurse said I had two types of malaria.

I noticed the door slowly open and a large golden tree kangaroo cautiously approached my bed. Behind her were several other marsupials from the jungle. They gathered solemnly around my bed—wallabies, cuscuses, sugar gliders—all the pets of my childhood, and then the great golden kangaroo spoke.

"We are here to bring you healing from the forest," she said, making a sweeping gesture with her chubby little furry arms.

"Ha! Nice to see you guys!" I said with a crooked smile from my feverish stupor. "Now go away," I moaned and turned my head toward the wall. "I know you're not real."

This wasn't my first time to have malaria. I was familiar with the strange hallucinations that accompanied the high fevers. I smiled. Even though they were imaginary, it was still nice to have visitors.

The tree kangaroo looked at the other animals in dismay.

"What do you mean we're not real? We're here to bring you healing from the forest."

"Go away…P L E A S E!"

"But we're here to bring you healing from…."

"Look," I interrupted the kangaroo's speech again. "First of all, there's no such thing as a talking kangaroo, and second, if you were real, the wallaby would have never made it past the chocolate cookies by the door."

The tree kangaroo looked offended. She put her hands on her hips.

The wallaby raised his hand from the back. "There are chocolate cookies by the door?!" he exclaimed as he looked around frantically.

"You can't have one," I said sternly.

Looking annoyed at the wallaby, the kangaroo snorted, turned back to me and continued with her sweeping arm gestures, "We are here to—"

Click. I snapped a photo of the furry nuisance with my iPhone and drifted off to sleep. Several days later when the medicine had kicked in I pulled up the photo and the tree kangaroo turned out to be Milli the golden retriever.

After twenty years, I had at long last returned to West Papua with my wife and my three girls for a visit. Aside from the "welcome home" reminder the malaria gave me, I was excited to show my children my hometown of Sentani where I had grown up, gone to school, and made so many life-forming memories. And it was good to be back with Uncle Wally and Aunt Joan for a while, as guests in their home.

I found West Papua vastly different from when I had last

been there. Shopping malls, Dunkin Donuts, Pizza Huts, and all sorts of development had taken place, though seemingly without any sort of forward planning the rapid development felt overwhelming. The roads were packed with motorcycles and cars; noisy shops had popped up on every corner, restaurants, and stalls of all sorts. The population was booming, the towns were hopping, and there was money flowing, which stood in stark contrast to the noticeable poverty that still existed there. On top of that it was Christmas.

Christmas in Papua. How can I describe that phenomenon? It's like baby Jesus takes on the Apocalypse. Every byway is crammed with *Pondok Natals* which are Christmas huts depicting the manger scene, but instead of a cute baby, the hut contains loud speakers which blare Christmas songs at an unholy decibel level night and day. Meanwhile, fireworks are apparently a must and millions of *rupiahs* are spent every Christmas on lighting up the sky with exploding colors. What month this starts and ends was unclear to me. My guess is that it lasts for several months 24/7 if anyone can get away with it. Silent nights there are not. Between the bustling traffic, the incessant fireworks exploding, the call to prayer from the mosques, the blaring Christmas music, Jesus in the manger and the stifling heat, well... I guess I was home.

I suppose it may have been hard for my children to understand how deeply moved I was to revisit the remote jungle outposts where missionaries continued to dedicate their lives to saving lives and souls. To see how these once forgotten tribes were now being educated, receiving health care, realizing their own dreams were now in reach thanks to the opportunities afforded through development and education.

A trip home wouldn't be complete without a return to the beach where it all started for me. My encounter with God. Where I really met him. Where he snatched me from the vast dark shark-infested ocean and the sea of hopelessness. Where I saw the light and for the first time realized how lost I had been. What a journey it had been. What an adventure.

Sitting on that familiar beach, looking at the stars, the smoldering fire, people I loved and who loved me, I felt complete. The warm air touched my skin, the sea lapped at my feet, my children slept peacefully by the warmth of the fire. Life for me began somewhere here, in simplicity, with all my questions. I had to lose myself to find myself. Lose what was broken and no good and discover something worth living for. I had found a beginning point; truth, life, purpose and meaning. I had found a way to know who God was and begin to unravel his good plan for me.

And as I stood under the starry sky and listened to the wind rustle gently through the palms, Uncle Wally came down to the water's edge. He was carrying our spearfishing gear.

We were older now as we looked at the dark water and the tropical night sky. The world had changed a lot. There were new dangers, new challenges, new adventures around the corner and I didn't know what was ahead. Uncle Wally was wading into deep waters with his work expanding education and healthcare to the indigenous people and I with mine in Fiji. Neither of us ever knew what we were going to face tomorrow but we both trusted our God.

There was a long silence as we stood and listened to the

waves roll in. Boom! Crash! Ssssss! Boom! Crash! Sssss! Oh that sweet, sweet sound. I breathed it all in deep into my soul. Sometimes it's just good to take a moment to listen. The sea beckoned and I was no longer afraid.

"Ready?" Uncle Wally asked.

I looked at him and grinned, "Yeah, let's do it."

EPILOGUE

Early in our journey together as a young married couple, Laura and I were approached to pioneer a Christian Community Development training center in Fiji. The project was aimed at developing a school to help train those who were poor in different technologies that would benefit them, physically, intellectually, and spiritually. Practical skills like construction, fish farming, agriculture and such. We agreed to join the team and within a few months ended up in the Fiji Islands, which have been our home ever since. We have worked with both those in poverty and western students in various capacities over the years.

Along the way, three little princesses have been born to us, Eden, Elani and Isla. All three were born in Fiji and know this country and call it home. When our first daughter, Eden, was born, tears came to my eyes as I thanked the Lord for letting me live to see my children. They are indeed even more exquisite, wonderful, and interesting than I could have ever imagined.

I know I am living on borrowed time, or perhaps "gifted" time. God has spared my life more times than I can count, and I know I don't deserve it. Why? Because he has a purpose for me. We all live on gifted time and he has designed a purpose for each one of us; a purpose that our unique experiences have prepared us perfectly for. The only thing left to do is to accept his plan for our lives and live in the peace of knowing we are doing what we were put on this earth to do.

To me, there is nothing worse than the thought that I'm not living a complete and fulfilling life; that there is somehow more to it all that I'm missing. And I don't like to miss a single adventure. When I was not in the place God has designed me to be—spiritually, emotionally, or even geographically—I suffered with that strong sense of being misplaced, my heart perpetually conflicted. When we reached Fiji, I knew we were where God wanted us to be.

The people of Fiji, who are world renowned for being some of the friendliest on the planet, have been wonderfully gracious hosts, and have become family to us. And while it has not always been like what you see on the postcards, it has been one of the great joys of our life to live and serve in this beautiful South Pacific nation we are now citizens of and call home.

It is life giving for me to be able to be in a place where I'm never far from my beloved ocean. I don't know what it is but it's something that's so much a part of me that it's difficult for me to ever be away from it for long. Perhaps I have saltwater in my veins now like my old friend Marawai whom I admired so much. We have a lot of visitors in Fiji and I love to see the wonder in their eyes when they get to experience the sea in all its glory. I like to go snorkeling with people who have never done it before and see how excited they get when they see the fish and coral. I love to take people sailing. And I even get to rescue a panicking tourist out of the water now and then and save them from drowning.

I had set my mind and heart on following Jesus, and there my affections have remained true. I've weathered many a storm, but I have not lost sight of the eternal beacon of light that is guiding me home. Whenever I have been enticed to abandon my faith (and I have been enticed greatly), I remember that night lost at sea. I refuse to go back there, deep into the hopelessness of my own heart and the darkness of my lost soul.

I know one day I will emerge safely on a distant shore; all of the dangers, the darkness, the fear, the hardships, and the tears behind me. Jesus will welcome me, maybe not in a robe but barefoot in beach shorts and carrying an extra surfboard for me or a dive mask and snorkel that doesn't leak. Not because I was perfect, and not because I didn't struggle and fail at times, but because that's just who he is.

ACKNOWLEDGMENTS

My warm and heartfelt thanks go out to the following people...

First of all to my tenacious editor and friend Kathy Groom whom I randomly found on the internet, who believed these stories should be written and pursued me across continents to get them on paper. Your positive enthusiasm for this project along with your husband Tom's has made it possible to get these stories out of my heart and into people's hands around the world. You are a godsend. I absolutely couldn't have done it without you. Thank you!

To my wife Laura and my parents who were always so supportive, as well as my friends who read it and gave me their input; I appreciate that so much.

And finally to all the young people who have listened to and loved my stories over the years: students, campers, interns, volunteers and visitors. Your great response to them has given me the inspiration to write them down. I hope you have enjoyed them. Now go have an adventure!

SCRIPTURES AND REFERENCES

The *Lucky Catch*
Have the gates of death been shown to you? Have you seen the gates of the shadow of death?
Job 38:17

The Creature
...when I looked for good, evil came; when I looked for light, then came darkness.
Job 30:26

Deep Calls to Deep
Have you journeyed to the springs of the sea or walked in the recesses of the deep?
Job 38:16

Deep calls to deep...all your waves and breakers have swept over me.
Psalm 42:7

Someone Is Trying to Kill Me
What is the way to the abode of light? And where does darkness reside? Can you take them to their places? Do you know the paths to their dwellings?
Job 38:19-20

Rapture Days
Can you bind the beautiful Pleiades? Can you loose the cords of Orion? Can you raise your voice to the clouds and cover yourself with water? What is the way to the place where lightning is dispersed, or the place where the east winds are scattered over the earth?
Job 38:24

When the Sharks Come
God has made my heart faint; the Almighty has terrified me. Yet I am not silenced by the darkness, by the thick darkness that covers my face.
Job 23:16-17

The Light
I am the light of the world. Whoever follows me will never walk in darkness, but will have the light of life.
John 8:12

A Time to Die
I assure you and most solemnly say to you, unless a grain of wheat falls into the earth and dies, it remains alone (just one grain, never more). But if it dies, it produces much grain and yields a harvest.
John 12:24

The Beginning

If you confess with your mouth that Jesus is Lord and believe in your heart that God raised him from the dead, you will be saved.

Romans 10:9